GW00499300

YOU ARE GOING TO F*CKING DIE

Adam Jones

© 2021 by Adam Jones

AJ1 Books, UK

ISBN 9798510007404

All rights reserved. No portion of this book maybe be reproduced, stored in a retrieval system, or transmitted in any form or by any means – electronic, mechanical, photocopy, recording, scanning or other, without the prior written permission of the authors.

Although the author has made every effort to ensure that the information in this book was correct at the time of publishing, and while this publication is designed to provide accurate information on the subject matter covered, the publisher and the author assume no responsibility for errors, inaccuracies, omissions, or any other inconsistencies herein and hereby disclaim any liability to any party for any loss, damage, or disruption caused by errors or omissions, whether such errors or omissions result from negligence, accident, or any other cause. The author makes no guarantees concerning the level of success you may experience by following the advice contained in this book, and you accept the risk that results will differ for each individual.

Table of Contents

SECTION 2 – LIVING & DYING   127

Disclaimer

If you don't like swearing or you're under 18 I'd recommend you probably put this book down immediately and pick up a Fearne Cotton book, no seriously I have heard very good things about them. As for this book; enjoy it, don't enjoy it, I don't really give a shit. I should really warn you that I write when I'm sober, I write when I'm tipsy and I write when I'm shitfaced on 13.2% Brewdog Stout and I've left most of the latter two efforts in this book, so you can see the full spectrum of me which I'm not necessarily proud of but not ashamed of either, why because eventually me and you are going to die so it doesn't matter two shits about our opinions in the long run. Also, the chances of you meeting me drunk are quite high so you may as well know what you're in for if you do. Below is a handy guide to see how many of each swear word I've used just so you can mentally prepare yourself for what lies ahead.

Cunt Count: 17

Shit Count: 174

Variants of Fuck Count: 214

Twat Count: 11

Bollocks Count: 12

Variants of Piss Count: 40

Variants of Wank Count: 4

Knob Count: 4

Bastard Count: 8

Dick Count: 11

FOREWORD

This is the second nonfiction book written by Adam Jones, also known to some people as AJ1. He is pretty convinced that if it was a thing when he was a kid, he would've been diagnosed with ADHD because he is so easily distracted...oh look a butterfly. He has a podcast called *The World According to AJ1* and a chatty one he does with his good friend Biff called *More After the Break*, a band called The Motive, a beautiful wife, and two wonderful sons. He loves KFC, swearing, investing, making money, playing guitar, drinking craft beer, playing with his kids, helping people, and writing books (including ones for kids) but not all at the same time or necessarily in that order. He loves his mom and dad and hates to talk about himself in the third person like he is now (yes, it's me!). His first book *The Money Mistakes of Mom and Dad* reached somewhere in the overall Amazon charts and somewhere else in the Amazon Business charts and he was chuffed to bits but not enough to dig through his screenshots to see where it placed.

His passion is to help people improve their lives whether it be financial, relationships, or wellbeing, while delivering this support in a frank, humorous, and irreverent way (basically he's a helpful prick!). While describing the book to his friend in a text message, predictive text interpreted 'self-help book' to 'self-*hell* book' which is probably more accurate than what he had originally typed. He started writing this before the Coronavirus madness kicked off but then during lockdown, lockdown 2: the revenge, and lockdown 3: the return, he found the time to complete it. You'll work out for yourself which bits were from when. Anyway, enough of this mystical third person bollocks; it's getting tiring, right?

Before you continue, I recommend getting yourself a notebook or journal and a pen to write down thoughts or feelings about what you read. I would also like you to join the Facebook and Instagram groups I have set up called 'You are going to fcking die' and @aj1Books so you can chat and post as you read. Finally, I suggest having a smart device like Amazon Alexa nearby as at the beginning of each chapter, I've put a quote and a song for you to listen to that (loosely) relate to the chapter, which I've conveniently made into a Spotify playlist called "You Are Going to F*cking Die" to make them easy to listen to. Who knows, it might become the soundtrack to your shower?. This will help you really immerse yourself in the vibe and get the most out of this book. No one reading (or writing) this book will live forever but I believe that by acknowledging this fact, it can set you free and help you get as much from the relatively short life that you have while you are here. Fasten your seatbelts and let's get on with the ride.

Memento Mori

This book is actually a 'memento mori' from the Latin phrase meaning 'a reminder of death'; something that you can carry, read, or listen to that acts as an aide memoir that you are mortal and eventually going to die, which in turn is meant to encourage you to take risks, appreciate your life, and not procrastinate. They come in many forms and could be a small skull or even a song that reminds you of this fact. Kind of like the totem in *Inception* that allows the dreamer to work out if they are in a dream or reality but this one is a little bit more morbid as it lets you know you're not immortal. Great tool but still a little bit of a pisser as well. I found a Latin verse on Wikipedia that was an old memento mori and pretty much sums up succinctly what I am about to show you in this book (only in Latin and without all the swearing obvs):

> Vita brevis breviter in brevi finietur,
>
> Mors venit velociter quae neminem veretur,
>
> Omnia mors perimit et nulli miseretur.
>
> Ad mortem festinamus peccare desistamus.

Which is translated to:

> Life is short, and shortly it will end;
>
> Death comes quickly and respects no one,
>
> Death destroys everything and takes pity on no one.
>
> To death we are hastening, let us refrain from sinning.

I know, I know it's not going to get into the Official Top 40 (if that's still a thing), but the message is still clear and a good one at that. I really like the idea of these memento moris (my spellcheck said Memento Morris, maybe he could be the mascot of the book lol) but I think it would be a bit weird to carry a small skull in your pocket, especially given the stop and search laws and the amount of paraphernalia you have to take to the shops nowadays (mask, hand sanitiser, etc.). I wonder what else I could use to remind me of the fact I'm going to die. I know, I'll put a cutout one at the end of this book with the title on, sorry it's less poetic way than the verse above. See! You got more than just a book when you picked this up—you got a memento fuckin mori motherfucker. Cut it out and Instagram me @aj1books with the hashtag #yagtfd so I know you're listening. Unless you got it on Kindle...but I guess you could always print it off and stick it in your wallet or purse, or somewhere you will see it every day, the fridge maybe, I don't know, I can't do everything for you.

By the way, while we're on about the title of this book, try to picture my conversation with the graphic designer on People Per Hour website asking a lovely woman called Norma to design the book cover. Luckily, she was quite understanding and, in my opinion, did a cracking job. Anyway, I'm getting a virtual 'look' from my editor to wrap up. Memento moris were designed to remind us that we are mortal and are going to die. Fast forward to now, where memento moris and their awesome weird lyrics are a thing of the past and it seems that the opposite is true: we actively avoid thinking about death, which has led to a certain level of apathy in our approach to life. People prefer to be bystanders and watch others than get stuck in themselves, so in my opinion, memento moris are needed more than ever and this book will attempt to fill the gap.

*Note since beginning to write this book a couple of things have occurred; Rob Moore (my writing hero) has mentioned MMs in his book and my friend Chris has sent me a link to a MM coin you can buy with a skull on it. Freaky!

Introduction

You Are Going to Fucking Die!

Do You Realize? – Flaming Lips

'On a long enough timeline, the survival rate
for everyone drops to zero.' Chuck Palahniuk,
Fight Club

Hello Sir/ Madam, your diagnosis is in, I have bad news. You are going to die! We all are – but the good news is not bloody yet...

Firstly, let me just stress this is not meant to be a serious book about religion or spirituality, so if you came here looking for that I'm afraid you've come to the wrong place and you should probably try and get a refund from Amazon, sorry. I don't really have a religion, but I respect the people that do and occasionally wish that I could put my faith into something that is unseen. I think that this would take a lot of the worry out of things that worry me, sometimes way more than they really should. Ok I believe that I'm not the one running the show here, as in I'm not god in the religious sense of the word, but I think that we as individual humans have a bigger part to play in the unfolding of our own lives than we know of or take responsibility for.

I believe that our thoughts combined with our actions influence what goes on in the world and if we can harness them then we can change our perspective which in turn could change our lives if we want or need them to.

I am not a psychiatrist, psychologist or a doctor, so the contents of this book should be taken with a pinch of salt whatever the hell that means, as these are just my opinions shared in written text as I guess most other books in the world are too. This book is part guide to wellbeing, part entertainment, part voodoo magic (joke), part rambling journal and part confessional and despite what I wrote in the foreword I do really hope that you get something from it.

Now we've got the ass covering unpleasantness out of the way, I already know what you're thinking. What a depressing and/ or aggressive title for a book?! Why would someone call a book that? And I should also say, if there are any police type people reading this, this is not a massive threat to kill the entire world via a book available on Amazon. I pinkie promise this is going to be a positive experience for all of us, honest. The purpose of me writing this is for it to be a direct wake up call to you (and me!) in order for us to start living our lives before it's too late. Yes, I know we're already living but I mean actually **_LIVING_** (look I used bold, capital and italics to emphasise it because I really want you to get the point). I mean as in living a good, fulfilling and enjoyable life. Not a life filled with insecurity, fear and endless scrolling through bloody social media (unless of course it's to read about me or my stuff)!

The transient nature of life and the reality of death I think for me, was most eloquently put by the Flaming Lips in their song 'Do You Realize' with the lyrics 'do you realise, that you have the most beautiful face? Do you realise, we're floating in space? Do you realise, that happiness makes you cry? Do you realise that everyone you know some day will die'? If you haven't heard it, please try to, it's good and I just managed to listen to it by saying 'Alexa play do you realise by the Flaming Lips on Spotify' aloud and hey presto it's on. Try it... but only if you have an Amazon device otherwise your neighbours and/ or family may think you've gone mental. We really are living in the future now folks, also what the hell does 'hey presto' mean?

Where was I? Oh yes, the point I'm trying to get to, is that we as a society hardly ever think about death which I think is quite odd because we are all going to experience it at some point (although the pandemic did for a little while put death front and centre of our minds). Covid aside, surely the fact that it is the only certain thing (other than birth) that links all of earths creatures after beating all of those other sperm to the egg, surviving child birth and then managing to stay alive long enough to be able to read this awesome book, we need to appreciate and maximise what little time we have here on this giant spinning rock. Simply put we are all born and we all die, what we do and experience in between these two events will never be exactly the same, not even identical twins experience exactly the same life. Birth and death are dead certs and link us all together. Yes, 'dead certs' is a great pun and yes, I'm including you in this generalisation Mr or Mrs Death Denial-Pants, which is a great name for a Mr. Man book don't you think? Note to self. Contact the Roger Hargreaves estate first thing Monday morning,

I'm gonna be rich!

I thought about death a lot when I was a young child, I couldn't fathom how the hell the world could carry on without me there to view it and this question still baffles me and melts my brain every time I really think about it even today. Which is the reason why I don't...often. Until now! Why lately? Is it a mid-life crisis? Maybe, I had just turned 40 when I started to write it, but also recently I had a bit of a health scare that coincided with me having a shitty time at work thanks to one piece of shit (a person, not an actual piece of poo). Essentially, I had an ache in my right testicle (the health scare not the horrible person) and I assumed (wrongly) that I wasn't long for this mortal coil (answers on a postcard for what a 'mortal coil' is). Basically, I thought I was gonna pop my clogs. Not that I own clogs or know what popping them means, fuck me it's hard for me to say this aloud or even write down, evidently, but I thought I was going to die. There I said it (wrote it), and I'm still alive, phew! That was a close one.

And maybe here lies the problem, I've feared dying so much that I don't talk or think about it and so when I do it's hard to articulate, and this in turn is why I think we as a society have become complacent with this gift of a life that we've been given and just possibly might be wasting our short time here on earth. For the purposes of this book I am assuming you are the same as me, in other words the more you look away from death the more you forget about the finite nature of life. And the more we forget the fact the more we forget to maximise the time we're here while sipping on the same skinny flat white in the same Caffe Nero, reading the same drivel on Facebook and moaning about Brexit or vegans or PPE for the NHS or whatever the media have hyped us up to be pissed off about this week. Regardless, we've forgotten to go on adventures, write symphonies, laugh heartily and cry until we can't laugh or cry anymore.

We've become sad and dull, and this (thanks for bearing with me) is why I believe that so many people are having mental breakdowns and the fact that suicide numbers have increased, and the ages of people being committed has gotten younger over the past 15 years.

It's almost like we've avoided and distracted ourselves from death so much that we've forgotten how to live, so we have created lives that are so boring because we're scared of ridicule or not being awesome or getting likes. This need for external approval and a lack of doing the adventurous, abnormal, interesting or risky means that we are missing out on life so much that we may as well not exist or indeed just die (please read that last sentence again aloud slowly). We've forgotten that we can put our phones down, delete our addictive apps, change where we live, our friends, our partners, our lifestyle, our job or whatever else we want to change and importantly we can change our thoughts and break habits that cause us these problems in the first place. We don't appreciate what we have because we don't acknowledge that we have it for a short amount of time and are sadly 100% guaranteed to lose it. Think the rollerblade scene in Home Alone for those of you old enough to remember the film, and roller blades for that matter. If you don't use them you'll eventually grow out of them and this is just like life, if you don't use it, eventually it will be too late to do anything with it. The mayfly has the shortest lifespan of any living creature on earth; they live for 24 hours, you don't see them settling down for a game on Fortnite, not that Nintendo have invented a Switch small enough for them yet. But you can see my point, why do we try and waste time, why don't we try and maximise it like our old pal mayfly?

I partly blame the internet as not only has it made the world feel like a smaller place because we can't escape it but thanks to social media everything we say or do is written down, photographed or recorded and unfortunately remembered and I don't think that that is very healthy for us as imperfect, learning and growing creatures. Because it is all recorded 'as us' for all to see, it is hard for us to change even if we want to. A photo of our exes can show up as a memory on Facebook at any random time of the day. We can see who's looking at us based on who we're 'friends' with and we're so fixated on looking at other people looking at us and looking good for them to look at us that we've stopped taking risks and the fun and spontaneity has disappeared from our lives or has vastly reduced because of this relatively new phenomenon.

Parents look at your children right now, are they on a phone or tablet? If they are walk over to them kindly ask for it, put it in the bin and go for a bike ride. Look at your friends right now are they drinking a latte in Caffe Nero on their phone while you're bored shitless? If they are, kindly ask for it and tell them they are shitty friends and that you want to go and build a dam in a local stream with twigs and shit. DO THIS RIGHT NOW! Oh, and if your elderly parents are on their kindles show them the title of this book and that should be enough to get a conversation started. Probably one that brings a 'tut tut' from them but at least they're away from their screen for five bloody minutes! Jeez.

I have conveniently divided this book into two sections; Life and Death, Living and Dying. Section One 'Life and Death' is about how we should approach our lives in light of the fact that we are going to die. Section Two 'Living and Dying' is about the acknowledgement of death as an actual thing and not something that might not happen. These are where you can apply the steps in Life and Death (get it!) to be less afraid of things and maximise your existence. The sections are quite loosely defined, and most chapters are independent of each other, so it lends itself to you picking it up when you're say on the toilet or a plane or a toilet on a plane and read random ones in any order. I shall warn you in advance that I also use lots of film references, common sayings and even some common sense. These are not meant to be patronising but to make them accessible to all audiences, and just because you've heard them all before doesn't mean that everyone else has so just run with them and take them as a guide to all rather than an insult to you.

You will also find a bonus mini book at the end called 'AJ1's Dadvice' which is a selection of random life tips that I have applied to my life and you might find useful to dip in and out of at will. Enjoy!

*Note if you are feeling suicidal and this is the book you've picked up skip straight to Chapter 22 Don't Kill Yourself (spoiler alert in the title there).

** Note if you are in an abusive relationship skip straight to Chapter 36 Abuse

SECTION 1

LIFE & DEATH

LIFE Chapter 1

Realise You Are Thinking

Wake Up Boo! – Boo Radleys

'The most important decision you will ever make is to be in a good mood' Voltaire

If you take nothing else away from this book, take away the title of this chapter, as this is one of the key realisations that helped me completely change my perspective on life. Why? Because when you realise that you are in charge of what you think you have more control over the types of thoughts you have and the lens you look at life through. Alcoholics Anonymous 12 steps begins with acknowledging the addiction, this is the same for thinkaholics, I am Adam Jones and I think too much. I even wrote a song for my band called 'Thinking Too Much' the first line is 'I can't let myself be happy'. I wrote that when I was a lot younger and it really was so true at the time. I denied myself happiness, because yes, you've guessed it, it's a choice and I analysed the shit out of everything including that very fact. 'But why am I sad?' Because you're thinking about being sad and not thinking about being happy. Like the drunk who's asking for another drink at the bar when he's already pissed, the more we do it the less we realise that we're doing it and that it can end up working out badly for us. Of course, we all think, but what does it mean to think? It's a term bandied about but never really thought much about outside of counselling and self-help books.

My thoughts about thought started to change about 12 to 18 months ago. I had downloaded an audio book on a whim, I had no idea what it was going to be about, and it looked like every other self-help book that I'd been digesting up until that point in time and I thought what the hell, may as well get that one too. I was expecting more of the same helpful advice but nothing life changing. Little did I know, that this was the one, the one I had been hoping for, the holy grail, the book that changed everything, the book that I'd been looking for, for all these years, the self-help book that actually let me help myself. You know the one where angel music plays, and Jacob's ladder shone down on it, you get the picture.

It was called the Inside Out Revolution by Michael Neill and this was the life equivalent to what Rob Moore and Robert Kiyosaki had done for me about money with their financial freedom books. It woke me up, slapped me in the face with a wet fish and made me smell the proverbial coffee. Now, if I'm honest, I can't accredit this awakening to just this one book, as I'd been reading a few others in a similar style at the time (hmm maybe it wasn't bought on a whim after all, what a lying git!) anyway the other books were as follows but probably not in this order; 'Little Book of Results' by Jamie Smart, 'The Courage to be Disliked' by Fumitake Koga and 'How to be F*cking Awesome' by Dan Meredith. Shortly after I finished Inside Out Revolution, I also read Neill's

'Super Coach' and 'Space Within' books. You could say I was binging on self-help, but I was having a right old shit of a time at work and needed some help desperately and thankfully these books were readily available for me to listen to on Audible.

All these authors, eluded to me the fact that you, yes you which meant me as well, have the choice about what we think about and how we react to our circumstances around us. Think about that for a moment (see I said think). Everything that happens to us is only made real by us thinking about what we have experienced. If we got run over and instantly forgot about it due to some crazy amnesia that meant we didn't think about our accident, then we wouldn't feel any different about our approach to road safety. But if we relive the event from our memories through thought, we may become frightened next time we're near the road. The thoughts have made a past event real in that moment even though the accident is no longer happening. Your reaction to the thoughts is simply that, your reaction, by thinking about it, you bring the memory and your reaction to it into your field of vision and if it's a negative, it can bring anger, worry or fear but if positive it can bring happiness or joy. By the way I'm not saying you should think positively about a car accident you've experienced.

I believe that our survival instincts have evolved so much that we can now analyse perceived danger and risk of death which makes us think about it too much and becomes counterproductive. Let me ask you what is the very worst thing that could happen to you? I'm guessing you said dying – ceasing to be, biting the bullet etc. So, avoiding death is useful right? Well yes but the only problem is sometimes in trying to protect us our brain goes too far, to the point where it renders us powerless and/ or makes us unable to see any positives through being too scared of things that probably won't kill us in this day and age.

Remove yourself from the modern world for a moment and imagine yourself as a caveman or woman. Your main goal is to stay alive and a big part of the way to achieve this is to belong to a community (safety in numbers/ hunting purposes etc), you crave remaining in this community (and being alive) so much that you start to calculate what is the best way to remain in it by thinking about it. Do I cosy up to the leader, do I make myself valuable or do I act vulnerable, so people look after me? Fast forward again and think of these scenarios in today's society. The sense of community, the desire to fit in and not be cast out, they are all there but magnified to the size of the whole world thanks to the internet. We have a desire to belong, but the internet is made up of the whole world and to please everyone my friend is one tiring (and impossible) thing to do. We must accept that we can't be liked by all and in some cases will probably be disliked. The next step is to realise that if someone doesn't like us, they won't kill us and that we (probably) won't die from it. Must think I won't die if someone doesn't like my book Adam!

If the thing that stops us doing something is ultimately the fear of death or more accurately the thought of the fear of death. E.g. the fear of being banished from society or some bollocks, we could waste our lives worrying about this fact through the act of thought. We will explore this more in the later sections but by accepting that we might die and moving forward with what we want to do anyway, as most things, there is a high chance that we won't die. If this is the case the thoughts (albeit designed to protect us) can be a hindrance rather than a help and removing them can set us free. As a quick reminder of what we say and what is true:

- We won't die of embarrassment (despite us saying we do)

- We don't die of shock (despite us saying we do),

- We don't even die of laughter (despite us saying we do).

The only thing we die of is death or more technically stopping breathing. If you can, I want you to realise that you are thinking. Then see thinking as just that, a thought and not your permanent reality. Try to remain indifferent to the present moment as much as you can and move forward accepting what comes your way with intrigue and curiosity rather than visiting (and comparing to) what has happened in the past or might happen in the future. Still with me? Good. Let's get on to what we can do now we know we only exist through thought with a bonus little cheeky swear word in the title of the next chapter. How controversial of me?

LIFE Chapter 2

Let Shit Go

Get Over It – OKGO

'Life is so short, why carry a load of shit with you?'
Adam Jones (Me!)

We as a species have been evolving for millions of years, from amoebas to the spoilt ass holes we are today. Along the way our brains have protected us by being able to work out how to avoid danger, find the good stuff like sex and food to the point where we're pretty self-sufficient which is great for us as a species. As the previous chapter states, when negative events happen to us it causes over-analysis of why we are scared, which is kind of like a D-dos attack on your brain. If you don't know what a D-Dos attack is Google it as it's something you may need to be aware of in the digital age, and I can't do everything for you. Anyway, I've had it where my girlfriend left me and caused me to stay awake endlessly working out what went wrong when what I actually needed was some facking sleep!

When things like this happen, you need to give a newsflash to your brain that the war against the dinosaurs is over and I'm sorry to say we don't need our tribe of cave men (community) as much to stay alive either so you don't have to be so fucked up when you lose a relationship or have conflict with someone anymore.

Today, the worst thing that could possibly happen to us will be something random like being hit by a drunk driver that we can't reasonably predict or prepare for. *Note this was written pre-Covid. So, if this is true, why do we worry about anything? Ok if you have bills that need to be paid to keep your home or have a child that needs feeding and you don't have any food, I'm not saying don't worry, of course not. But for things like relationship problems or lack of perceived success at work or your friend has a newer car than you, I have a two-word phrase that has really stood me well and here it is; 'fuck it'. Simple but effective don't you think?

Now don't get me wrong it doesn't always work and sometimes saying 'fuck it' can make things worse for instance saying that when you need to brake on the motorway as you're hurtling towards a massive artic lorry, probably won't do the job (PS I was today old that I realised an artic lorry has nothing to do with the Arctic and freezing the contents lol). But we have to start to acknowledge that these thoughts are just that; thoughts, and here's the worst part about them but also the key to setting you free; the more you try to fight them the more they will dig themselves in like a little fucking splinter in your thumb. The more you get the tweezers on it the more you push it in so you can't quite get it, whereas if you left it and accepted the pain and discomfort and ignored it for a little while, did something else to distract yourself, time would pass and it would eventually come out of its own accord and heal on its own. Instead, we mentally pick at the thought, analysing want went wrong, Google it, read books about it, meditate on it, bore our friends to death about it and we wonder why we can't stop thinking about it. Spoiler alert BECAUSE YOU NEVER STOP THINKING ABOUT IT DUH!!

I used to love the sitcom Friends and there's a scene where Ross has realised that the whiniest person he knows; Janet, has become sick of him whining. This revelation makes him instantly snap out of his fug. He was dwelling on the past relationship and forgetting that he could move on to the next one with relatively little effort and pissing everyone else off while talking about it, leading him to be boring and dull in the process and ironically but predictably ruining his chances of moving on and finding someone else.

This is what we're doing when we have our little rituals, such as mantras and meditation and in some extreme cases OCD-like activities that we think are helping us but are actually doing the opposite. The very act of trying to pre-empt and push against our unwanted thoughts, the more we are thinking about them and their consequences and causing them to manifest harder and stronger in our minds. I'm not saying meditation is a bad thing, far from it, I'm just saying if you're only meditating to solve a problem then it probably won't work for this very reason. As that thought will be the driver and be in your meditative state and cement it even more than it was before. The less we try to change our negative thoughts the less we think about them the more chance we have of them fucking off permanently. Think about it, if you're alive and reading this, so far in your life there's nothing you haven't overcome – so worrying has worked right? Wrong! You've probably wasted energy spending time worrying about them unnecessarily. A nice example of this type of thinking was demonstrated in the The Simpsons, where Lisa convinces her Dad Homer that a rock keeps tigers away because she has the rock and there are no tigers about. Just because you do one thing, and something comes about doesn't always mean it's because you have or haven't done the thing. Ps I have some meditation rocks for sale if anyone wants them. LOL.

Michael Neill in his book The Inside Out Revolution advocates acknowledging living with the uncomfortable thoughts whilst telling yourself that better thoughts will come. If you cut yourself, you stick a plaster on it and wait for it to heal, you don't analyse it night and day, trying to push the skin to heal together, your body does it naturally, the same principle applies to your brain and its' thoughts, so we need to get ourselves to this point when we're hurting mentally.

I've found the trick is to realise when you're doing it because so many times in the middle of the night I feel that all is lost and worry the shit out of myself, the next morning new thoughts have turned up and I feel much better. If I could work out that it's *just* a thought mid-worry, then I would be able to think it'll be ok in the morning and then I would be able to get to sleep quicker and arrive at the morning refreshed. Just because you think something once, it doesn't mean that that is all you will ever think, and that that is your thought process for the rest of time, you don't have to own the thought or keep it and as long as you can keep calm and not react with loads of analysis or action during the pain of shitty thoughts better ones will come along eventually and you can get on with more constructive stuff like taking over the world or whatever else you get up to in your spare time.

So how does this link back to death and indeed the title of the chapter? Well it's very simple really. I have found that most, if not all my negative thinking that I have had throughout my life has been caused by holding resentment to other people for something they've done either to me or someone I know. Yes, it is painful when someone hurts you or betrays you or just downright pisses you off, however, holding on to that negativity is bad for your wellbeing and frankly a waste of your short time being here on the planet. The title of this chapter is 'let shit' go and my advice is do just that, I have seen friends and family waste years of good times on grudges only to regret it when it's too late and one of them has passed away. In the words of the Dalai Lama 'holding a grudge is like drinking poison and hoping the other person will die', the negative thoughts are in you and not them, so forgive them, let it go and move on. Let's get on with the next chapter, shall we?

LIFE Chapter 3

What Has Happened to Us?

Video Killed the Radio Star – The Buggles

'Wherever you are, be all there' Jim Elliot

As I mentioned in the introduction, I'm here writing this book to help by waking us all up out of our dream state that we've all seemingly slipped into over the last 10 years since the advance of Skynet, I mean Apple and Facebook. I believe we are all (myself included) lost in our pursuit of things that may not be beneficial or our ultimate purpose on this massive ball of dirt we call home (that's earth if you're reading this on Mars but I guess the principle is still the same, but well done for being brave and changing planet you probably don't need this book!). Here is a quick example of how stuff has changed since I've been alive, I remember going to see Oasis back on their 'Be Here Now' tour in 1997, yes, I remember it, and it is a memory that I hold in my brain to draw up on whenever I want to reminisce. I saw it from underneath two swearing Mancunian men's armpits covered in Carling from jumping up and down uncontrollably, and the glimpses of Noel and Liam were magical.

Now when I go and see a gig it is from behind a mobile phone, mainly mine but also other people's, hundreds of em. In fact, there are so many screens in front of me, I may as well have watched it on the bloody TV at home as at least I would have got one version of it filmed from a decent pissing angle rather than wobbly, poor quality clips that sound like a bee stuck in a tin can. My question is. Why am I recording this moment? Why is everyone else? Is it because I/ we have a terrible memory? I do but that's not the reason I do it. To show someone else? No because the person I'm most likely to show it to is standing next to me (wifey). To watch at a later date for pleasure? No because I can't remember ever purposely watching one of these shaky shitty quality videos of these bands I've recorded or anyone asking me to see them. So why the hell am I recording this moment? Please don't say it's because everyone else is, come on Adam please. No, it's not that I don't think. Is it because I can? Is it to maximise my ticket price investment by having a souvenir or is it that we want to remind ourselves that we were there, we existed, we got out of the house and went to a place and then, sadly shared it on social media? Fuck, this is a darker book than I was expecting to write but keep with me.

Either way, as I type I'm realising that I don't need to record the moment as more than likely some other saddo will have recorded it and put it up on YouTube and better still unlike back in the day, digital photography has meant that most things of note get recorded professionally and published anyway. My point is, unlike the Oasis gig where I experienced the gig for myself to remember, I'm now not living the gig, I'm living me recording the gig so I'm now a camera man at a gig rather than myself. Are you doing this?

Memories are so much better than videos, they can be magical, they can be told like a story, they can be kept secret, and memories stay with you until you die and don't need to be stored on a cloud or depend on your battery being charged to access them, although I'm sure Mark Zuckerberg has got a secret plan for that in some dystopian future where you take a shit on Facebook Live. Incidentally, I watched the Oxford Cambridge boat race on TV over the weekend and below the camera from the grandstand three camera phones were also recording it! Why?! Surely you can see the giant fucking camera behind you and surely you understand that you will get the same footage on Iplayer in better quality when you get fucking home you thick piece of shit?!?

I think if we're honest with ourselves it comes down to our desire to show off, don't give me that blank face, come on you know. We do it for the likes on social media, we record our experiences to post them on Facebook so other people can witness what an awesome fucking time we're having at festivals and gigs, while others are at home looking at Facebook, proving to our 'friends' that we never meet in real life that we do stuff and maybe just maybe we might have a better life than them, even though it may not be true. This would be fine, but then we go back and check the likes, and refresh to see if we've had anymore, all of which is taking away from our experience of the event itself that we've paid our hard earned cash for. It's like we are projecting a life rather than being present in a life, in the context of death, why the fuck do we bother? I'm here to say don't, live the moment, fuck what other people think and then you'll be happier, it may not be instantly but in the long run if you stop comparing yourself and maximise the moment you'll thank yourself, rather than constantly keeping up with the Jones's and I know for a fact you can't keep up with me LOL.

Calm down Adam. I am going to attempt to get to the bottom of where things went wrong for us as a society and how we can all wake up and smell the coffee without taking a picture of the cunt. Yes, I wrote cunt not 'can't' or 'Clint' I dropped the actual C bomb and if you're offended by my language you may as well just fuck off now. Sorry, not sorry. It's a word, a piece of language and if it offends you so badly you better get back into your cotton wool bed and hope that nothing bad happens because guess what, as the Flaming Lips said, 'we're floating in space', one day we'll be hit by a giant rock and a few 'cunts' and 'fucks' will be the least of your worries.

Where was I?! Oh yeah. To be fair, I guess we as a society do think about death occasionally when we watch it happen on films and dramas and hear about folks dying in other towns and villages around the world and occasionally a member of our family passes too. *Note during the Coronavirus we have a lot of death on the news but in 'normal times' we don't have it as a regular occurrence thankfully, also the government made a great effort to dehumanise the number of deaths by giving us other stats such as the R-rate, so we continue to ignore the inevitable. Therefore, I think this book is (luckily for us) perfectly timed as we 'cautiously but irreversibly' get back out of the plot of Shaun of the Dead.

In 'normal times' we don't often think about our own mortality that often, well I don't until writing this book and if I do it's never usually in a positive light and I think that that's one of the reasons why there's so many problems in the world. We're so caught up on social media bullshit, listening to people bitch and moan and watching drama unfold that we've forgotten that there's a real life on a real planet with real people going on outside our window, that we can if we choose to go and experience up close and personal. Think back and apart from maybe a few weird times, tell me how many good memories you have of reading Twitter or Facebook or any of the other social media shatforms. I bet you can't, now tell me what memories do spring to mind from going out? Meeting people? Doing actual things other than sitting on your fackin' phone. Yes, I thought so. And why is that? Because it's real. It's not fake, it's not text or an image of some prick from school showing their perfect family or some silly cow at a party or whatever, instead it's you doing those things which is a) less passive and b) less depressing. So next time you are slipping your hand into your pocket to get your phone out to record the gig, pause and think do I really want to record this moment, or shall I just fucking enjoy it and store it in my long-term memory?

LIFE Chapter 4

Selfie Generation

Girls on Film – Duran Duran

'Don't let others decide who you are' Denis Rodman

From the moment my first son was born, he was snapped like a celeb by the paparazzi on mine and his mom's mobile phones, happy, sad, ill, awake or asleep we put a camera phone in his face to capture every minute of his being alive. Which is understandable right? You've made the miracle of life why wouldn't you want to capture it? My youngest has recently arrived and me and my wife have continued the same tradition of taking more pics of him than if the real Elvis walked into a Las Vegas photography convention. I'm ok with it because I don't think that we are alone in this behaviour, most parents are ready with their hands on their pockets ready to grab their phones out like John Wayne pulling his gun in the wild west, at the mere mention of their child's name, to show their latest capture of their offspring. There must be quadrillions of baby images floating above us in the cloud, but this indoctrination into their own mini paparazzi lifestyle leaves little wonder as to why so many people in younger generations grow up obsessed with taking selfies and probably more worryingly focusing on themselves more than others and desperate for that next attention fix. Which are conveniently enabled by things like Snapchat, Instagram and more recently TikTok.

It's gotten to the point now where people are more concerned about how they look in the photo over and above the landmark or attraction that they are (allegedly) there to see. While on a recent trip to Devon's Miniature Village I saw two girls take 10 or so photos to get the perfect photo of themselves, looking at each one and adjusting their pose to get, well I don't know what, to get the right angle possibly. I mean it wasn't the pyramids or the Taj Mahal (well not full size anyway lol) it was a miniature village, their appearance on I'm guessing social media was paramount over their time and enjoyment at the attraction. I also remember being in a beautiful square in Prague having a beer with friends, a guy and his, I think girlfriend were recording something for social media and he was having a right go at her for not making him look good. I mean they were in an amazing location and all they were seeing was a tiny screen with that arrogant prick on it! I'm all for social media and its marketing benefits but surely we have to realise it's getting passed a joke for fucks sake.

So, what to do about this? Well of course I am not saying don't take photographs or attempt to get a good one when it counts. I still remember the days where we had one shot at a photograph because film and developing was so expensive. My dad used to keep the films in their little tubs in the fridge for some reason and then wait for a Prontaprint envelope to arrive to send them away and then wait what seemed like an eternity to get them back. Invariably some would be excellent, and some would be utter dog shit. Utilise the technology that you have at your fingertips but enjoy the moment too, make it a good experience first before making it a good photo. The picture should be an afterthought, only just remembered not the main fucking event, unless you're a photographer and it's your job, then you should absolutely focus (pun intended) on getting the best shot!

LIFE Chapter 5

Live Your Best Life

Tub Thumping – Chumbawumba

'You are confined only by the walls you build yourself'
Andrew Murphy

Are you living your best life? Do you know what your best life is? I'm not sure I do, I know I like certain things and I know when I've had a good day but couldn't possibly say if this is my best life or not. I have a friend at work called Deborah, she's a ball of energy and whenever she's out she's always living her best life. She really doesn't give a shit about what people think of her and fair fucking play I wish I could be like that. She probably does give a shit because she is not openly rude or offensive to people, she's not a psychopath. But she definitely has the mindset to make sure she is pleased first even if that means going against the grain of the group that she's with. Does this make people dislike her? You'd think it would wouldn't you, but actually she is very well loved in our organisation and has a far-reaching group of friends outside of work too. Most people's instinctive response to group or peer pressure is to follow the crowd and go with the majority regardless of what you think or feel about the activity. I think we do this instinctively, so people will like us. People such as Deborah have an inner confidence that allows them to be satisfied with their own choices regardless of who else wants to join in and then this is compounded with a not giving a fuck if it's the wrong choice personality, that allows her to always be 'right' and happy no matter what the outcome of her own or someone else's actions. Incidentally, I have just read this paragraph to Deborah and she was surprised that I thought this way about her. She was pleased she was in the book but always thought of herself as a pleaser. I guess this beautifully illustrates the difference between the perceptions of ourselves versus the perception that others have of us.

So how do we get to live our own best life? Well for me it comes down to several factors, I've already touched quite a bit on the power of our thoughts, but I think to be more specific I think it comes down to how we've been bought up that has influenced what we think. Our parents have a desire for us to have friends and be part of the community, whether it be school, family or our local neighbourhood and in doing so they encourage us to share with others and do things that will make people like us for example doing what the majority want to do. However, I personally think that this has gone a little too far where we almost encourage our children to be weak and submissive to the more confident ones. I used to hate it when my little one would play on his own and not part of the group, I realised recently this was a strong thing to do and I shouldn't have been as forceful to make him play what the group were playing. This sounds more dramatic than what it was. I thought he would struggle making friends by not playing the group games but in fact he was doing what he wanted to do, so I was stopping him living his best life. In the end I just gave up out of frustration but looking back I am proud of the little bugger for having his own mind, today he has a lot of friends, so my tinkering may have helped, who knows? It's interesting that I gauge having lots of friends as a yard stick, this must come from my parents influencing me to want to be liked, curse those lousy beatniks *Simpsons reference.

Did your parents do this to you? Do you feel that you follow the herd now to keep the status quo? If you do, try to identify the moments that you do. I'm not saying change your behaviour (yet!) but just notice when you would prefer to be doing something else while doing something you don't necessarily want to do so as not to annoy someone or at least keep the peace. Next, I want you to think about what the consequence would be if you were to say no to doing the activity or at least declining politely. What would happen? Would you be in danger? Would the person shout at you for not doing it? Would they not talk to you? Or would it be that you would fear missing out?

Well, if you would be in danger – my first reaction would say that you need new people in your life and you should probably call the police or local authorities as no fucking body should be touching you because of something you don't want to do. If you're not doing anything illegal or harmful to others (e.g. not looking after your own child) you should not be harmed and even then, it shouldn't be harm you come to, I guess.

If the person would shout then this is similar to danger, the relationship is probably not very healthy, and I'd advise not being in a relationship/ friendship with them for much longer if this is a regular occurrence. Same for not talking to you but sometimes I guess people can be stroppy and get over it which is less of a worry for me. See I do give a shit about my readers.

The fear of missing out was probably my biggest one, I got myself in a lot of debt going on holidays I couldn't afford just in case I missed out on something. But what was I fearful of missing out on? I didn't realise for a long time that my being there or not does not change my experience. By not being there does not mean that I am not anywhere. I will still be alive when they are there and when they come back. I don't just vanish while they have a great time, and they don't vanish from contact either. I'm assuming some of this comes with age but if you're young I want to give you this bit of knowledge now. If you don't want to go or you can't for some reason, do not worry, your life doesn't end if you don't and no matter how good it is, or the pictures look, they are still themselves while doing it and you can have equally as good a time by yourself or with someone else by doing something else instead. Also, the compounding effect of debt to pay for something you can't afford can cripple you for a long time after the event is over, but that's another book!

Be like Deborah, don't want to do something don't do it, do want to do something do it. If you don't like the friends you've got, find new ones, it's never been easier to find new and interesting people that will respect you for you rather than the you that goes along with stuff to stay friends. Live your best life not someone else's!

LIFE Chapter 6

Groundhog Day

Right Here, Right Now – Fat Boy Slim

'I think every day is Groundhog Day. I get to learn from my mistakes and be better every day' Ashton Kutcher

Have you ever seen the Bill Murray film; Groundhog Day? Well if you haven't, I recommend you do. It's quite dated now as it was released in the early 90's but I love it as it's hilarious and if I think about it pretty fucking similar to Coronavirus lockdown conditions in 2020. Over and above that it has great life lessons for us all to learn from. For those of you that haven't seen it Murray's character experiences the same day over and over again and cannot escape the current day to get to the next day in other words tomorrow. Just imagine living the exact same events repeatedly. After the initial shock and realisation that not even killing himself can end the madness, his character starts to make the best day out of the one he's got. He learns new skills, saves people's lives and makes himself a town favourite, and even manages to get Andie MacDowell to fall in love with him, yeah right, I love Bill Murray as much as the next man but that ain't happening in real life so I'm calling bullshit on that one. She's still looking hot all these years on by the way!

Anyways, the astute amongst you have already probably seen where I am going with this, that we can, and I believe should, take lessons from this premise. In my podcast I often talk about living in the now and appreciating the moment you're in, rather than regretting the past or worrying about the future. This is the youngest you will ever be again. So, make sure you seize the day. The moment you finish this paragraph, that moment will never come back again. Every day we wake up is potentially the last one that we will experience and it's also an opportunity to start all over again despite what has happened to us yesterday, the day before, months or years ago. Why not make your life what you want it to be?

I saw on the news the other day some silly cow wanted to be a mermaid when she grew up, guess what she was now doing for a living?! A postman...no silly bollocks she's a fucking mermaid. I mean what the fuck?! Fair play to that nutcase for following her random dreams and wearing a sleeping bag round her legs to the swimming baths every day for money. Where oh where did I stop following my dreams? I work in an office and guess what, AJ1 aged 7, that little bastard was not wishing to be in an office, he wasn't wishing to be a fucking mermaid either but hey. What I was wishing to be was a mad scientist vampire. When does that stop? When did it stop? Probably the day I also realised I'll never travel back in time or be invisible despite what 80s teen movies had told me. Fucking shit 80s films, I'm sorry I love you really!

You can be or do whatever it is you want to do, the only person stopping you is you. If you can't be arsed to do a 30-minute workout and not have a take away every night, then I'm sorry to say you will always be overweight. Conversely, if you do magic tricks every day no matter how bad you are at it, you can call yourself a magician. I'm currently calling myself an author!

Back to Groundhog Day; Bill's character Phil starts to learn lots of new talents while trapped in the same day, he goes to piano lessons and becomes an expert blues pianist, learns to ice sculpture, rescues little old ladies who've broken down, saves kids falling out of trees, saves a homeless man's life and countless other things. Why is that different to what we experience? If you think about it, it's not that different really. We are also trapped, in the same day over and over (yes, we call it something different and may have different weather or people in it), but we have the same body and the same brain more or less as yesterday and probably tomorrow but like Bill we never get to tomorrow or go back to yesterday, we only have the right here and right now. So why do we choose to sit on our fat fucking asses and play stupid shit games on our fucking phones (after writing this I have just decided to delete a really addictive game off my phone as I'm missing out on my little family growing up)?

Why do we procrastinate; why do we put off learning the piano or ice sculpture or whatever? Because we always think that we are going to get another day to do it.... But guess what? We, me and you are going to die, one day we won't be able to learn the piano, this could (but hopefully not) be our last day on the planet, and how did we spend it, well thankfully I wrote a bit of this book, but I also spent an hour on that shitty pissing game. Arghhh silly twat! What did you do today to make you feel proud? (Try reading that without singing it like Heather Small!).

Does this scenario sound familiar to anyone, alarm goes off, snooze for 15 minutes, drink water next to bed, get a cup of tea and a piece of toast or cereal, drag yourself to the shower, brush your teeth, get dressed (probably smart casual), go to work do X on a computer, go for a Costa or Café Nero or a Subway (insert overpriced brand here) for lunch, return to work, and live out the afternoon waiting to get home, return home, maybe go to gym, maybe have a drink, maybe watch an ITV drama, maybe have sex, maybe have a wank, go to sleep, wake up and repeat? Now this is my existence too and there's nothing wrong with this, except I don't wear smart casual and I don't eat breakfast but what I am doing that I think is probably slightly different to most, is I am following my dream, no not the vampire scientist one, the dream of being an author, I'm writing this book dummy. I truly believe that everyone has got something like this inside them, not necessarily a sweary self-help book but something that they are good at or something that they'd like to be good at. I am not sitting here writing manuscripts every day like the guy at the end of the credits at the end of Murder She Wrote, but I do sit down every so often outside of my own Groundhog Day and write words like this one here 'bum', here's another 'tits' and one final 'bollocks', living the dream peeps living the dream! I also do other shit too, like being a frontman of a band and the world's laziest podcaster, think I'm averaging one every four months at the current tally.

You need to find out what it is that lights your candle? What gets you out of bed and active and doesn't feel like work? If you have a passion, then follow it, keep doing it over and over until you're good at it. If you're no good at it today, try again tomorrow and the next day and the next day. Don't give up and one day through the power of practice and compounding you will have made improvements and be quite good at it. If you stop after the first hurdle cause it's too hard then you'll never know. What is the point in being alive if you're just going to sit there existing and doing fuck all with it? Don't laugh, I'm Joe Pesci serious on this. Don't give a shit what other people say, they're just jealous that they're not doing it and you might actually achieve something or they're boring bastards criticising you because they haven't got passion for anything like you have. Fuck them, fuck them all!

*Note can you tell I wrote this chapter when I was drunk? No? Shit I must act like I'm pissed all the time then or I'm a right miserable old cunt and I hadn't realised. Either way ho hum. On to the next chapter!

LIFE Chapter 7

Choose Life

Choose Life – PF Project

'Choose life. Choose a job. Choose a career. Choose a family. Choose a fucking big television. Choose washing machines, cars, compact disc players and electrical tin openers. Choose good health, low cholesterol and dental insurance. Choose fixed interest mortgage repayments, choose a starter home. Choose your friends. Choose leisure wear and matching luggage. Choose a three-piece suite on higher purchase in a range of fucking fabrics. Choose DIY and wondering who the fuck you are on a Sunday morning. Choose sitting on that couch watching mind-numbing, spirit crushing game shows, stuffing fucking junk food into your mouth. Choose rotting away in the end of it all, pishing your last in a miserable hole, nothing more than an embarrassment to the selfish, fucked up brats you spawned to replace yourself, choose your future. Choose life...

But why would I want to do a thing like that?'

– Renton from Trainspotting (Irvine Welsh)

I've quoted and referenced a lot of films throughout this book, but this one is possibly the most meaningful to me as it arrived into pop culture and my life during a very influential time. I was 16, and to quote another film; Point Break I was 'young, dumb and full of cum' just started at college and this was where my life started changing. Up until that point I'd been a boring little shit. I'd go to school, come home, and be totally scared of everything and everyone around me (that was my victim Groundhog Day existence then). I believe I was like this as I was bought up primarily by my mom, my dad was a bakery engineer who worked shifts, which meant I didn't see him that much as he slept a lot during the day. My mom worried about everything and wanted to protect me from the world (which I guess all moms do). She saw danger everywhere and in turn so did I. When I got older I started to interact with my dad more as for some weird reason he only worked about 5 days every 9 years and I realised he was (and still is) a pretty chilled out guy, he did not give a fuck about anything or so it seemed. It turned out later he did give a fuck but never wanted to show me or my mom which I kind of respect but wish he'd showed it as it would've made me feel less uptight and bad about my own tendency to worry. Anyway, compared to my mom it was like he was smoking 7 spliffs a day, the guy was relaxed, get it? And I realised if I compared both of my parents' lives, my dad's life was so much easier. I mean who actually wants to give that much of a fuck about anything, not me at 16 and not me ever since.

Don't get me wrong, occasionally things get to me and lockdown and Coronavirus bollocks got to me big time but everyday life, is really a walk in the park. Why is this? Why have I got it so good now? Because at the tender age of 16 I followed Irvine Welsh's advice, I chose life. I decided that if I was here, I may as well live. Up until this age I didn't do things through fear of being hurt or upsetting my family (my mom mainly). I decided to change all of this and do what I wanted to do because I realised my mom would deal with whatever happened to me and her fear should not be a reason for me to be scared. I had realised that if I didn't do what I wanted then, that one day I would look back and I'd have wasted all of my time here and I was more scared of regretting this fact than the fear itself.

Trainspotting was so influential as I knew the characters in real life, not the same people but the same type of people and I knew I needed to break the monotony and really live. Renton, the lead character attempts to breakaway from the negative characters that have filled his life up until this point and this is something that we all need to do occasionally, shed some of the deadwood. Make sure that the people that surround you are how you want to see yourself, do they have the same morals as you? Do they have the same goals and desires as you (more on this later), the reason why I'm asking is because my favourite author Rob Moore suggests that you end up becoming the sum of the 5 people that you spend most of your time with? Are THEY who YOU want to be? If they are not it's time to make a change, it's time to choose life. And before anyone writes in I know that the quote in Trainspotting is meant to be a tongue in cheek look at the commercialism at the time but there is a strong message of breaking free from the drudgery of everyday life and making something of yourself, so step away from your inbox and calm down.

Finally, for this chapter I want you to picture yourself 20-30 years in the future or even at your death bed, what do you want to look back on, is what you're doing right now (outside of Covid circumstances) what you want to see? Are you proud of what you've been doing in your life? Make a list of everything that you'd like to see and/ or be said about you. Now look at where you are now and what you are doing. Are you doing things that will lead to this outcome? Are you following your passions or at least taking steps towards following them? If you are not, then I want you to start thinking about how you could change these things. What is the first step that you can do immediately to start to achieve them? Want to write a book? What's it about? What type of book will it be? Want to learn an instrument? Which one? If you've got one pick it up and play, get on YouTube and start learning. The key to doing anything is starting, don't wait until a near death experience like me or for tomorrow or another day, start now. Fucking do it, DO IT NOW!

LIFE Chapter 8

Kick Yourself Out to Play

Round Are Way – Oasis

'Kids don't remember their best day of television'
Unknown

When I was a kid I had a Nintendo Gameboy, even writing those two words makes my internal 14-year-old hum the Tetris theme and remember endless days fixated on that 2-inch square green screen. My mom and dad had given me this item and I'm not sure they had realised at the time that they may as well have given me a crack pipe for how addicted I got to that seemingly innocuous piece of cream coloured plastic. I fucking loved it, I mean LOVED IT! Arghhh. Before continuing to my point about this early addiction I must confess that I completely see now why they were so frustrated with me on it, as I have totally dropped a bollock and made the same mistake they did and gave my little lad, a Nintendo Switch shaped crack pipe for his 7th birthday.

What the actual fuck was I thinking?! Idiot. I only get him every other weekend and now I only see him for 10 minutes out of a 48-hour weekend and this is just to do his homework (this is an exaggeration and it's not an actual crack pipe before you phone social services!).

So back to the point in hand, my mom and dad spotted this addiction and decided enough was enough and realised that they had to take action, they couldn't afford rehab, so they used to kick me out of the house to play with my friends. 'Look at the sun out there, and you're sitting in here' they'd say, 'you're wasting your life on that thing' and fair play to them they booted me out to find someone to play with and boy how I resented them for doing that to me. I was having so much fun on my Gameboy, I didn't want to go out and face the real world with the inevitable real people that I'd have to engage with. I mean I did live in a relatively rough area, so I see my 7 to 14-year-old self's reticence to go out and 'play' which could easily have been replaced with 'occasionally be beaten up by some Tipton blokes'.

But, and it's a big but I look back and am glad that they forced me out to play, yes it was rough yes there were dicks but I also made some lovely friends, I met girls, I built dams, I played postman's knock (sorry), I drank cheap cider over a field, I smoked a pipe with tobacco in it, I sang Wonderwall with my arm round a group of chaps, I played tick, I played football (though I was crap), I built tree houses, I cooked bacon on a park bench that we'd set on fire, I swam in a canal, I drove my bike down a fucking steep hill and fell off it, I broke up fights, I forged friendships that still exist all these years on, all of which gave me life experiences and made me who I am today. If I'd have stayed in and played Super Mario Land or whatever my latest game was, I'd have missed out on all those real-life memories, all the laughs helped me grow. I also dare say would be a lot more scared of life now and probably become a recluse. Yes, it's true I didn't want to go out, but I'm so glad I did which proves the point of this book that life is for living not for sitting and watching.

Yes, I understand that the advent of the internet means that communities can form online and I'm sure friendships and memories can be formed but don't do this in lieu of getting out there in the real world, let your kids outside for fucks sake and importantly, let yourself out, force yourself out if you have to and experience real life. I don't want my son to go out further than in front of my house because I can't see him or control the environment he enters, but I also need to realise he needs to spread his wings and fly from the nest otherwise he'll never stand on his own two feet, meet girls (or boys), drink cider in a park and all that other shit that didn't do me (much) harm.

Black Mirror has a great episode where a mother installs a chip in their daughter and blocks her from seeing or hearing anything scary or bad and gets addicted to watching and protecting her to the point where her daughter has grown up and she still meddles in her life. Fucked up. When my first child was born, I had an audio baby monitor, so I could hear him if he was distressed. For my second child, technology has moved on (or at least got cheaper) and we have a camera monitor for him, I have already had discussions with wifey about at what point we turn the camera off. Let your kids out, they have phones they already have more than I did when I was younger, and I definitely had more than my dad and his friends had to look after him 'they used to send us out with cold tea and sandwiches and we wouldn't come back until it was getting dark'. You can wrap your kids and yourself in cotton wool but (and this is really hard to write as a father) you and they are going to die one day, and you both need to live lives and generate memories for when you're too old to do stuff. Don't deny them this by taking the easy option and leaving them on their devices and you get off yours too. Besides which there are also (sometimes darker) dangers on there too. Anyway, why are you still reading this I've told you to go out and play, I'll catch you tomorrow for the next chapter.

LIFE Chapter 9

Work to Live or Live to Work?

22 Grand Job – The Rakes

'We need to do a better job of putting ourselves higher on our own to do list' Michele Obama

There's a famous anecdote probably from John Lennon or someone like that, that goes 'no one ever says, 'I wish I'd spent more time in the office' on their deathbed' and this to me is so very true. Where I work there are a lot of committed people getting in early and staying late even when there's not that much to do, I see them sitting there after everyone else has gone home despite some of them having partners and children. I often wonder what is keeping them there? Maybe they struggle to complete their work in the allotted time? Maybe they want to appear to be committed so they get an end of year bonus? Maybe they have a passion for their work? Maybe they don't like their spouse? Or Maybe they just don't have anything else in their life? I doubt it's about getting overtime as I work at a place where we are lucky enough to receive a salary, a decent one at that and work flexibly so we get paid as long as we get the job done, not the number of hours we put in. Don't get me wrong, if there is an emergency or something that needs prepping I'll come in early or do a bit in the evening or over the weekend to get it ready/ finish what needs to be done but this is the exception and not the rule. I once called two of my direct reports to a meeting and asked how I could be leaving work and they be staying behind every night, was I giving them too much work? Did we need a bigger team? Turns out they both just wanted to get ahead for some upcoming leave that they had but my message to them was clear. If you can't do what I've asked within the day, then we need to rethink what I've asked you to do.

If you are one of those people that does more than your contracted hours, remember every minute you work over you are reducing your hourly rate. As well as that you are also setting a precedent for your manager that you can achieve more within your allotted 37 hours so will always expect more even when there are special circumstances that require a late evening, early morning or weekend day. Obviously, this may be different if you are a contractor or self-employed, but you still need to have an eye on the amount of time you spend at your laptop/ on the job. The term work life balance is not one that should be thought about lightly.

I suppose if I look back to when I first started my working career I would go over and above what was necessary, and I guess you could describe me as a bit of a brown nose. This was mainly due to me not getting a job straight away when I left uni and I was so grateful for being given a chance (albeit at an exploitative wage) I felt I needed to repay them in some way and avoid being back in the dole queue which I bloody hated. But now as a slightly more cynical, middle aged, married father of two I have realised something fundamental about work. My home life (family and friends) are much more important, why? Because work is always and will always be there waiting to be done, effortlessly present anticipating my return to it. Our jobs/ income generating opportunities are less willing to accept lack of attendance or interest compared to our families which maybe the reason why we slip into focusing on our jobs and take those close to us for granted (until it's too late). I have realised that I need to put effort in to seeing and really being present with my family and friends to keep the relationships alive. If I kept checking my work emails when I was out with my friends, missing key bits of the conversation and ducking out for more pressing matters, I'm sure they'd tire of this and probably stop inviting me out. As I've mentioned, my eldest doesn't live with me so in order for us to bond it is paramount for me to be 'present' when he comes for the weekend even if he is distracted by Fortnite or some other game on his Switchpipe.

I am acutely aware that when I die, work will carry on and they will replace me with someone or something else that maybe better or worse than me. My family will hopefully see me as irreplaceable. I loved my last job at the fire service because I really felt I was helping and making a difference, my boss; Mick was very complimentary and we felt like a team but when he retired, the new guy replaced him and my hard work was, in my mind, not as appreciated and I had to start again so I left, and guess what someone equally good took my place. This happens all the time and no matter how important you think you are, you can pretty much always be replaced by another model. Yes, even you! Now just for the record I'm not advocating taking your foot off the gas, rolling up to work smoking a spliff and telling your boss to fuck himself in his own ass but what I am suggesting is developing a healthy work life balance. Key word here is balance. It's time to wake up peeps, you are only here on the planet once, and you only have so many hours left to live.

I think we all assume that we have plenty of time but in Matthew Michalewicz's excellent book 'Life in Half a Second' he suggests we think this because we gauge our time on what's already passed (our age), rather than counting down and monitoring how long we have left. He says if the average person lives until they are 80 and therefore, we (excluding extreme circumstances) can assume that that is when we will live to as well. Then, by subtracting our current age from this, so if you are 40 you have 40 years left and if you multiply that by 365 (days in a year dummy!) we find out roughly how many days we have left, in this case, 14,600 days left on the planet. Sharpens your focus seeing it as days doesn't it?! Some days drag, and some days fly by, but these are ticking down now, even while you read, and I write this. Scary isn't it?

That report can wait, your family will only be this age once, your kids will only want to play with you for a short period of time before they grow up and find sex, drugs, rock and roll...oh and in my sons case video games. *Note I am currently forcing myself to learn how to play Fortnite, so I have something in common with him).

The moral of this chapter is, don't waste your life thinking that your place of work will collapse without you, it won't. Or that they will drop to their knees and thank you for saving the day at the end of 50 years they won't. Or that they will hesitate firing you if they need to cut costs. I once worked for a public sector company that faced a huge cost cutting exercise. The first message that came out from the Board was 'we're all in this together'. The first decision that the Board made was 'we will not be looking at the Board for cuts', charming. This stinks but survival in the work place is as rife in the public sector as it is in the private, and if you were in that position, you might think of acting the same.

If you do find yourself working all of the hours that god sends, you are more than likely avoiding or missing something fundamental somewhere else in your life and it might be time to close your laptop, go home and work out what the hell that is before it is too late, remember you are going to fucking die and you don't want that to be alone in a cold office on your pissing laptop do you? Oh, you do? Well fill your fucking boots then.

LIFE Chapter 10

You Are Here

How Good it Was – The Courteeners

'What you think you; you become. What you feel; you attract. What you imagine; you create' Buddha

Before you read this please note I had not taken a massive dose of LSD and listened to Jimi Hendrix before writing this, I had a couple of beers last night and that's it. Promise.

You ever been at a beach, theme park or a museum and there's a big map with a fucking massive arrow pointing to where you are on the map with the words 'YOU ARE HERE' next to them? For me this is a convenient reminder for us all that we are somewhere...always even when we're asleep, even when we're drunk or depressed or happy or overwhelmingly in love or in agonising heartbreak...we are here. And that is what I want to talk about. I've just been meditating (yes I do this despite being from Tipton) and although I was meant to be completely focused on my breath, my mind was racing so I was trying to do the mindfulness technique of 'body check', this is where you acknowledge and sense your body parts to remind yourself that it's not just a movie through your eyes but you have limbs and skin and shit that all play an active role as well which brings you into the present moment hence the term mindfulness. While trying to do the final whole-body sequence, I said to myself 'you are here' and that was that. This chapter was born, I knew I was going to write it.

From a thought during meditation and a bit of cheeky mindfulness these words now exist on my laptop screen and soon to be on paper or kindle and now in your hands (hopefully!). So, what did I mean, 'you are here'? Seems obvious that I was there and currently you are here physically in existence reading this book and being awesome and I'm off somewhere else being me, swearing and probably not being as awesome. But we don't often acknowledge that we are here, on a planet spinning in the solar system being held to it by a mysterious force called gravity. We don't acknowledge that we exist, we just exist. We were once a sperm that beat its mates to a giant egg, we were born through a vagina (or maybe a belly), we were fed milk by our parents, we were taught things (good and bad) by grownups, and we breathe oxygen, eat food and drink water to be alive. We have blood running through our veins and we have, even though we don't think about it often, opportunities all around us. We have a life to live and we are the architects of what we do (mainly) through our own choices.

Our existence is now and now only, by being here there's also something else that's true, we are not anywhere else. We're not living in Back to the Future because as far as I know scientists haven't managed to invent a time machine where we can be in two places at the same time, so wherever we are is the only place that we are or can be. We can't leave our bodies and the brain we have is the one we're stuck with forever, no swapsies, whether you like it or not, so you may as well become friends with it even if you don't necessarily agree with it all (any of) the time. Incidentally, this is the same for your looks and appearance too.

And by the very nature of the above, conversely once you are not here, you are not anywhere and that's fine too. In the words of the Courteeners; 'She was here and now she's gone, never to be seen again'. Why have we as a society forgotten the fundamentals of life? We are born and eventually we will die and what we do in between those two events is up to us. It's a choice, I can choose to sit on my arse and watch Netflix eating lard. I can choose to go out and do something good in the world, I can choose to write this book. It's all my choice, but what's the point in being passive and doing fuck all with this awesome life simulator we find ourselves in? Because someone might laugh or criticise us. Boo fucking hoo, let them laugh and criticise it doesn't matter a shit. What's worse? Someone laughing at you or dying inside watching everyone else live their fucking life how they want to while you rot on a sofa in your pyjama bottoms? If you're not happy, change your thoughts and then your actions will follow, if you're happy wallowing put this book down grab another can and put your fucking feet up! Oh, and change your pjs you stink of fucking piss!

As an aside, during lockdown we learnt to do the simpler things in life; we as a family went for picnics in the park, flew kites, went fishing, built tree houses, had BBQs and went on endless walks. We could've sat in the house, but where's the fun in that? Remember when all is said and done and you're an old fart in a hospital bed, the only thing you will have left are your memories and maybe a few photographs to keep you company. Do you want them to be of skydiving and laughing with your mates, or do you want them of you scrolling through Facebook being offended about something that has nothing to do with you?! WAKE UP BITCHES! Unless you are being mistreated or you or someone you know is in serious danger just enjoy your life, don't search for something to be sad about, what's the point when you could be happy?

I'm definitely not saying ignore shit happening on your doorstep or ignore people in need around the world, I'm just saying don't dwell on all of the negativity that the media spews out to get you wound up because guess what there's more of the cunts doing the same thing to someone else with the opposite views to you. I think actually most people (apart from a few psychos) can get on with most people regardless of colour, creed, sexuality or fackin political views even if secretly they disagree with you. The earth is huge avoid the cunts you don't like and hang about with and enjoy the rest. So there! And all because I thought about YOU ARE HERE. You are here, it's your choice where you are next, so make it fun or at least not shit.

LIFE Chapter 11

It's All about the Journey, Man!

Get What You Give – New Radicals

'Everyone wants to live on top of the mountain, but all the happiness and growth occurs while you're climbing it' Andy Rooney

The world has never been more open to us thanks to cheaper travel costs and the internet and soon space will be open for business too. But there is one fact that travelling anywhere will not change, you. Wherever you go (even in a virtual simulator of someone else), the only thing for certain is that you will always be there, and you will always be you. Regardless of the plastic surgery you have, the filters on your Insta account or the avatar you created in Roblox you will always have the same brain and the same thoughts. When you dream of leaving, and you imagine a new sexier you I'm sorry to tell you that that is a complete impossibility. The only way of even remotely changing yourself would be to have a brain injury and even then, the you that you are then won't be the you now, so you would have different thoughts and desires to what you were changing for in the first place. Yes, take a look in the mirror, look behind your eyes, that's the brain that your mom cooked in her belly and the one that you've been destroying with alcohol, drugs, films, TV and porn for the past couple of decades. It's fine though because there's some great news, you're not broken. Let me just say that again YOU ARE NOT BROKEN. 'But I am 'cause loads of bad shit happened to me', yeah and?!? Loads of bad shit happens to everyone, but it's all relative, the only difference is how much you or they think about the bad shit that happened to them.

Everyone who is successful has had shit happen to them which is possibly, no probably why they've had the drive to be successful so less bad shit happens to them now. If you want your life to change, don't wish to be someone else, wish to be a better version of you and then make it happen. You have the choice, to turn your life around. I can't make you do it same as a personal trainer can't do the exercise for you, but we can show you the way. Listen man (or woman) this is a onetime gig, you've got endless possibilities with what you can do. Honest, they may not be apparent as your life might be covered in shit at the moment (hopefully not literally but you get my point!) but they are there. You can achieve anything you want to achieve, and if you don't achieve it the journey would *still* be fucking awesome.

See the bit that I hadn't realised during my life until recently, is that the thing that you want to achieve isn't the best part. We say to ourselves, life will be better when my band is signed to a record label, or life will be better when I get the girl/ boy, or life will be better when I get the new job/ car/ whatever. However, when I have achieved some of the things I've been wanting, you know these singular pinnacle events of accomplishment, they haven't been as rewarding as I was expecting them to be. Bit of a damp squib really, (and yes, it is squib, not squid like some idiots say). Usually, the best bit of the achievement has been the anticipation and the work towards the goal, you know the journey. If instantly everyone could get all the money and all of the things they ever wanted, life would be extremely boring wouldn't it and this is really my main point here, your life is not about you immediately being gratified it is about you striving and achieving something (as you not someone else) and then even if you don't achieve it you (and only you) will have experienced juxtaposed highs and lows that make the 'trying to achieve it' worthwhile and rewarding. *Note I have recently learned the term for this continual aspiration for new things, it is called the Hedonic Treadmill, Google it.

My own real-life example of this is my band. I've been in bands now for 24 years (wow!) and we've had some minor success and record label interest, however my original goal for joining the band was to get signed and be as big as Oasis with me as Liam obvs. However, once I started playing in the band, I realised we had to practice, write and record songs and play gigs to get heard, it then developed that doing these things was what I enjoyed doing and my motivation to continue as I got older. We'd have a laugh at practice, I loved crafting songs and the recording and gigging were just good excuses to show how far we'd come and have a good old knees up with our mates. At the time of writing we haven't been signed (boo!) but the journey we've had, and the near misses and laughs has become the joy and the story. Instead of regretting not being signed I am proud to say I am in a band and enjoy the individual moments along the way despite having not achieved what I set out to do originally. I never say never but as it becomes increasingly unlikely that we'll top the charts, I look back and think well what if we'd have instant success when I was 16, and got signed, would the journey have been different? Would I have the same wife? Would my children be different? Possibly. One of Richard Curtis's romcoms called 'About Time' eloquently and cheesily shows how small changes could lead to different outcomes check it out.

Also, would the tour buses or the press have been annoying? I also have to ask did I want it bad enough? Did I try hard enough? We all had full time jobs, none of us gave them up to pursue the dream. But even those questions are part of MY story no one-else's and that's the beauty of it. The moral of the story is to appreciate the ride rather than what's at the end of the journey as that's just a moment in time when it's all over, the here and now is real so maximise it before you wake up one day and you don't have any story because you were too scared to start any journeys.

If you keep chipping away at whatever it is you want to achieve regardless of what society or other people make you feel about it, is key to a happy life. If you're over 50 and wish you were a footballer, keep playing as long as you can. If you can't compete choose a lesser team, become a ref or a coach, start a blog or a fanzine. Keep following your passion, you never know what successes may arise. If you want the perfect partner, that's not a problem, define what this looks like (rather than guessing each time you see someone) and go on dating sites that allow you to match personalities and keep going until you find (near) perfection, maybe go for about 80% to make it interesting. Nothing is written in stone, that says you have to settle, and if you keep going long enough you will have met enough people to know what you like and dislike. If you end up single at the end of that journey, then you have your memories of all the dates and probably a few hundred cats to keep you company lol.

I should also heavily caveat this with that it's ok to change direction too, if you decide that you no longer want to be a footballer and want to join a pottery club then that's fine too. Maybe combine the two and make pots in the shape of footballs. I was watching an old interview with Billy Connolly last night and he said 'you need to find what you were meant to do' this really rang true to me. Be who you want to be, do what you want to do and the things that make you happy life is too short not to.

LIFE Chapter 12

Funeral Selfies

Smokers Outside the Hospital Doors – Editors

'Grief is the price we pay for love' Queen Elizabeth II

It's kind of strange that I sat down today to write about this story and it turns out it is the anniversary (or near enough) of the event itself. A few years ago, my uncle Keith passed away. He was a real-life genuinely natural cool person, he lived the rock and roll lifestyle despite not being famous, was loved by virtually everyone he met and like most rock stars sadly died earlier than he should have. He lived a full life and while growing up he was my hero! Interestingly, when I was younger I was surprised to find out that his hero was my dad, you know the one I wrote about in the other book. When I think about the stories of my dad in his younger days, I can understand why, but my dad eventually settled down with my mom (Keith's sister hence him being my uncle duh!) and became a normal dad, and in a not so strange quirk of fate he's now become my hero but for totally different reasons to what my uncle loved about him and I loved about my uncle. I hope you understood all that, as it was a right bitch to write.

Anyway, I digress, Keith's death itself was a very scary event in my life but just before it all happened something quite funny happened. I hadn't seen any of my family for years, as I had got distracted with girls, alcohol, bands and working in order of preference. And in that time, I had grown into a man (they were living their lives too, so I don't feel that guilty). On hearing the news that my uncle was ill in hospital I went down straight after work to see him, still in my suit and tie. When I got there, I was greeted with open arms by relatives and it was a lovely experience albeit in sad circumstances. My aunty Sue (who's awesome by the way), showed me into Keith's bed on the ward where my uncle Mick; Keith's brother, was sitting looking very low. I sat next to him quietly. He nodded his head. I nodded back. He said, 'so, how is he?' and I replied, 'I don't know I've only just got here'. He looked at me puzzled and my aunty turned to him and said, 'It's Adam you prat' to which he replied, 'fuck me I thought you were the doctor god you've got old and bald!' we all laughed but I was a bit gutted about it (mainly because it was true), but thankful that it took the edge off the situation.

The scary part came later that evening after most relatives had gone home. Aunty Sue and I had stayed back to chat as we'd always got on when I was younger, and I'd offered her a lift home. She asked if I'd take her to the pub for a quick drink to calm her nerves once I'd finally convinced her to go home and get some rest. We drove to the pub ordered the drinks, no sooner had we done so, Sue's mobile rang. It was the hospital, we looked at each other worried and Sue said, 'oh god'. They needed us to come back immediately, as Keith had 'gone'. I'm sure I probably broke the speed limit back, doing a five-minute journey in two, we ran through the empty hospital and ran on to the ward and there was my uncle sitting bolt upright with his eyes open and his chest breathing. We asked why they called us, and they said, 'Keith has passed' and we were like 'no he's there breathing', our hearts pounding from the ill-advised running and both of our years of alcohol abuse. 'No, he's gone, I'm sorry'. They closed the curtains 'but, but his eyes are open and his chest' Sue pleaded. 'That is just the life support machine, I'm sorry' replied the nurse coldly.

We walked away, we sat in the hospital lobby for 10 minutes. My aunty called someone to tell them the news and I called my mom to do the same. We both stood silent for a good five minutes afterwards shocked at how much life had changed since ordering the drink at the pub and how messed up it was that we witnessed Keith's bizarre but strangely apt exit. To this day we still talk about it and how it fucked us both up and probably should've sued the hospital or some crazy shit like that but to be honest it's been quite cathartic to put this down into words in this book so thanks for indulging me. However, this is not the purpose of the chapter though it does serve to remind us of the books title as like Keith, YOU ARE GOING TO FUCKING DIE.

The point of talking about Keith's death is something that happened a year or two later, when I looked at a photo of the wake after the funeral. Now, I'm not proud of my actions at this funeral, frankly I was a massive bell end! I was going through a breakup with a girl I thought was the one (she wasn't) and I thought getting off my tits on Jack Daniels and Coca-Cola was going to put the death and the relationship clear out of my mind (it didn't). It was my uncle's local and it was a small pub with a pool table, and a dartboard. My uncle had put some money behind the bar from the grave (fuck knows how although he was a grave digger at one point so maybe he'd picked up some tips from the dead!). There was a nice buffet and some 'interesting' characters as he'd led a full and eclectic life. I got talking to two lesbians, it's not really of significance that they were lesbian, but I wasn't sure how to put it down that they were together, and I wasn't chatting them up or anything. We were drinking like fuck and at one point my dad said he saw me open my wallet out to the barman and offered everyone in the whole pub a drink. If you've read the other book you know he wasn't impressed with this. Incidentally, that night I had a hankering for a kebab and a mini fish and so made my mom and dad drive me to a pizza shop to try and buy one. A fucking pizza shop for a kebab and a mini fish after my mom's brothers fucking funeral! Told you TOTAL.BELL.END. Sorry mom although I did ask you not to read this book, so I'll say sorry in person when I see her next which is hopefully soon.

Ok get to the point already! Am I talking to me or am I saying what I think you're thinking? Don't know. Either way, time passed, and life moved on and then one day about a year ago I was flicking through the gallery on my old phone and there is a picture of me standing at the bar, pissed with these two women, I clicked the picture to zoom in and I saw something that deeply saddened me. Behind us on the torn red leather seats in the pub lounge was my Aunty Sue crying her heart out. I mean sobbing with a tissue towards her left eye and at that moment when I saw her distress it hit me like a cold bucket of water. I had never seen a picture of someone I knew actually really crying. Yes, of course I've seen babies crying or people acting as if they're crying but I mean real tears from the grief of losing a loved one. Sue adored Keith, and this was evident in this moment of solitude captured in the background of a drunken photograph. It was also at this point that I realised that the reason I have never seen a picture of someone crying is because no one takes them. No one would go up to Sue or anyone at a funeral and say, 'Say Cheese', no because a) you would be a heartless cunt but b) and probably more importantly no one wants to capture a memory of anguish and despair. Why? Because it's not nice to see and though I have seen Sue since, the emotion she felt on that day was real and know in my heart that Keith will always mean a lot to her. We all book photographers for our weddings, christenings (if you have them), etc but I'm sure photographers don't get booked for funerals very often if at all.

It was this realisation that snowballed into my thinking about social media, when I'm on it (occasionally) there's loads of people smiling back at me, showing off their pets or new garden or holiday snaps but no one is ever putting their break up photos on there or the time they trod in dog shit. AND here's the key part because you only see these happy clappy snapshots wrapped up with a 'all is fucking ace' one liner you assume that their life is fucking awesome and yours by comparison sucks. Meanwhile, you live in reality including the times you stub your toe, or a child is screaming so loud next door that you can't sleep, that you start to believe that your life is actually pretty shit. Now for the record, I'm not saying that these folks are not happy but there is a danger that we look at their seemingly idyllic, Insta filtered lives and assume that they are living in constant bliss while we go through shit stuff including pain and heartache. It was when I realised this point that I immediately started to reduce my use of social media in fact I think I came off it completely for a good while after.

I returned to social media eventually and one day recently my wife questioned why I liked a photo of someone who I'm not that keen on because she knows I'm not that keen on em and thought it was hypocritical. Why was I mindlessly and passively liking someone packaging their lives up for Facebook to show how good they can pretend to have it when there's a whole world of people, places, food and activities to experience in the real world including and especially with my own family right there in the same room as me?! You can do this too, I'm not saying quit all social media, it is part of modern day life and can be a fun and interactive experience, my suggestion is to limit your time on it to say half an hour a day and when you do see posts, remember that these people have to take a shit as well and they're not living any special celebrity airbrushed lifestyle like they're making out. If you're feeling like certain people, make you feel worse about your situation why not try muting them or blocking them and only visit them when you're in a good place. You never know though, if you live your life outside of social media you may not feel the need to be on there, flicking through in the first place. Whatever you decide to do I feel the need to say 'go get em tiger! Grrrrrrr'...Sorry about that.

P.s If you don't believe my ramblings about social media being the devil, don't just take my word for it, go on to Netflix and watch The Social Dilemma, amongst other things, the founders and designers of these apps admit that their algorithms are designed to provide you with your own personal feed of news tailored specifically to you. This is not because they're really nice people that run these companies but because they want to get you addicted to them, so they can make money out of you. A key line that stuck with me was if the tool is free, then you are the product being sold to advertisers. Scary isn't it? They're making money out of you feeling like crap.

LIFE Chapter 13

All That Glitters

Stars in Their Eyes – Just Jack

'In the future everyone will be famous for 15 minutes'
Andy Warhol

In the words of Take That 'today this could be the greatest day of our lives' or then again it might not be that good and that's ok or, it could be bloody crap and that's ok too. If it's not the best day, don't worry as it doesn't matter because (hopefully) there are plenty more to be had all of which could be super ace unicorn riding farting rainbows awesome or an absolute smeg and cack sandwich bad. There was a study that analysed the handwriting of suicide notes (wow, they must've had nothing better to do). What they found was that there was a lot of disappointment (obviously) but moreover they were more disappointed because they had higher expectations about what their lives were going to turn out like. Basically, these people had assumed that their life should have been better more of the time. It could be surmised that they had killed their self through sheer dissatisfaction with the hand that they'd been dealt but the life that they'd wanted wasn't necessarily ever going to be achievable. Nowadays, everyone is the star of their own show on social media, everyone has a channel, which is fine but not everyone can be super famous or have something special happen to them as by the very definition of fame or special, if lots of people achieve it, it ceases to be special or fameworthy. Mind blowing, I know!

I'm sitting here writing this in a cottage in Somerset drinking a can of JD & Coke (mmm!) assuming that I won't be Stephen King or even Rob Moore, but I am writing it because I want to write a book. Back in the day when I joined a band I thought I was as cool as Liam Gallagher and had the song writing skills of Noel and it hit me hard when I realised I wasn't and haven't and I was probably never going to play Wembley. I've often contemplated that these fantasies that mainly men seem to have are the reason why there is so much mental health problems (and suicides) in men over 40, maybe the boyhood dreams of being a footballer like Ronaldo or an astronaut are dashed at around this age and the subsequent alcohol abuse, and mid-life crises ensue. I did believe, until writing this book that women had more realistic expectations for life but according to my editor she has found women have similarly heady goals for their lives including but not limited to 'man of their dreams', 'perfect kids' and so on. So perhaps it's more of a human condition to over expect.

I'm sure you'll be pleased to hear that I have some advice on this matter. Take each day as it comes, yes, I know we have to, but I mean try not to expect anything either terribly bad or super good. Take a stoical approach to what arises, what does this mean? If something happens that could be perceived as a negative occurrence do not dwell or complain about it but simply accept it for what it is. Also, don't be too over emotional when things seemingly good happen. Try to concentrate your feelings down rather than having big emotions either way, accept what happens to you and then move on to the next event. I originally wrote be indifferent, but this is more than that, it is simply accepting what life gives you without assigning an exaggerated emotion towards it. If someone cuts you up on the road accept it, assume that they are in a rush and move on, if someone gives you a compliment assume they are being polite and move on. The less you place on these moments the less you will either be disappointed if someone is negative towards you and/ or less angry you'll be if someone seemingly disrespects you.

You have no idea what goes on in people's personal life, same as people have no idea what goes on in yours, so they have no clue that you didn't get a good night's sleep, had a break up or a family member die, so forgive them for treating you as if nothing happened and try to be kind to other people if they are a shitbag to you occasionally. *Note this is not a reason to accept bad behaviour though.

Whether you achieve your dream or not, just remember you are still you and there is always another chance to win or lose again right up until the point you stop breathing. The trick is to keep moving forward to what you want and never give up on your dreams and aspirations no matter what life throws at you. You are you and the best thing that you can ever be, and I'm sure there are plenty of people who will love you for that very reason, so don't give up on life, if at first you don't succeed and all that bollocks. You may not achieve superstardom, but you are the star of your existence and really that should be enough, if it's not ask yourself why it isn't? Do some soul searching to see why you're seeking approval from strangers and question yourself if you are prepared for the negative as well as the positive feedback. The only person you need to please is you it doesn't matter what anyone else thinks.

LIFE Chapter 14

Happily, Ever After

Movies – Alien Ant Farm

'Life is not a movie so stop waiting for someone to
come around and write a happy ending for you'
Richard Davis

Bad news peeps, the fairy tales and films are bullshit!
You know at the end of the movie, when the hero
and his or her lover drive off into the sunset after a
massive ordeal, the next morning they have to wake
up and go to work, look after the kids and put the bins
out. Hollywood has been lying to us, by conveniently
putting the credits up to signify the end, they've lulled
us into thinking that all that action has led them to a
life of complete bliss. This has led some of us to expect
that from our lives. But bliss is a fallacy, everyone
yes EVERYONE has down days, everyone has to do
something they don't necessarily want to do. Despite
what people post on social media (and you all know

what I think about that) these blissful people have moments that aren't so great, maybe even shit things happen to them. You may think, if I'm rich I'll have no problems, or if I get the girl/ boy and I'm not single I'll have no problems. But each success that you have will just lead to a different set of problems down the line, obviously some worse than others. None the less the problems don't disappear, same as all of our movie hero's' problems wouldn't disappear, just because the baddy is dead or whatever.

You get loads of money, you have to worry about hanging on to it or sharing it out or not looking like you're rubbing it in. You get the girl or boy and they may not be all that you thought they were or may want you to change in some way, you get the perfect house in the perfect street only to find Jonny and Jilly Shitbox have also moved in next door! Noooooooooo.

Brandon Flowers the lead singer of The Killers said something along the lines of the only easy love, is new love. Basically, he was saying that after the initial throes of a brand spanking new relationship where the adrenalin and passion flow like Lambrini on a Newcastle hen do, after this, normality kicks in and you have to work at the relationship. This can also be applied to new jobs, new houses, new cities, new children. Everything starts off with a kaboom of pleasure, the excitement of the newness but eventually the shine wears off, newness fades into familiarity and you (if you want to keep it being good) will have to work at enjoying/ keeping what you've got. Reminding yourself that new is not necessarily better and the unknown is no better than the familiar at least not in the long term.

I know this sounds rather bleak but it's actually a positive, it means you can stop fantasising about the next big thing that you do and appreciate what you've got. Chill where you are for a little while rather than craving change. And where does this desire for change arise? It begins when you start to compare yourself to other people or past and/ or future self. You are so desperate to be somewhere else that you forget that you are here right now and though it may not seem like the movies, not even the actors who play the heroes experience complete and utter happiness. In the context I think Covid has been a great leveller, where money couldn't buy a way out of it and this has allowed people to be happy at home and grateful for what they had there, as no one has been able to experience any different. I hope this feeling remains with people into the future when Covid becomes less of an issue for the human race. Just remember the old clichés (not another one) the grass isn't greener on the other side, it's not getting want it's wanting what you've got. In other words, stop comparing yourself with other people (or even your past or future self), appreciate that there is always someone worse off than you that would be grateful for what you have right now. Yes, even you!

LIFE Chapter 15

Being Old Sneaks Up on You

74-75 – The Connells

'Forty is the old age of youth; fifty is the youth of old age' Victor Hugo

This chapter is to tip you off that time is ticking on whether you like it or not and whether you realise it or not. Since the age of being able to work out how old I feel, I have always felt younger than my age sometimes up to 10 years younger (although not when I was 10!). Now, at the tender age of 40 I feel about 35 and that's great for me because I'm giving myself 5 years under my actual age. Incidentally, I have met people that have acted what I would describe as 'old' at relatively young ages. Sometimes even in their 20's they have this unsettlingly mature head on their shoulders, this paragraph kind of excludes you if you think you might be one of those odd youngy oldy people. You're not odd really, I just wanted to see if you were paying attention. So yes, I feel in my mid 30's in my early 40's and that's good but more recently, occasionally things happen that make me feel my age or even slightly older.

For instance, today, I went for a walk with my wife and son to try to get him off to sleep, we didn't walk very far but after about 20 minutes my knee started to twinge. Now we weren't walking very fast or up any steep hills this was just a flat 'normal' walk along the road. Why was I twinging? I'm only 35 (in my head) and I'm not what I would describe as fat. Other stuff happens too, you start to be the oldest in your social group or workplace, right now you might be the youngest but give it enough time and you'll be celebrating some young person's 21st and you'll be crying in to your 'Naughty at 40' mug, it will happen to you, it's inevitable. What do we do about this unsurprising surprise fate that life gives us. It's worth saying the twinges and 21st's don't happen all of the time and I drift back to being between 32 and 38 but the point I'm trying to make is that despite how young you feel and act we are all aging by the minute. Also, and you may not believe this, time seems to speed up as you get older, Christmas's and birthdays arrive again shortly after you've just celebrated them, and you are left thinking shit another year has passed. This phenomenon is a stark contrast to how long a year or even a day at school used to seem to take.

Luckily for me I have never been sporty so my clicky knees haven't made me reconsider my desire to be a sporting hero like David Beckham but thinking about it may be the lack of sport in my life is the reason they click. Not sure but what I do know is, they didn't click walking up the stairs when I was younger and now they do. Pisser. My lovely friend Mark, he's roughly my age and he lives in Ireland, recently posted on Facebook that for the first time ever when visiting the doctor with an ailment, that the doctor gave his age as the problem rather than attempting to prescribe something to help fix whatever it was. It comes to us all and it will come for you. Don't forget this, if you're in your 20's take every opportunity that your young muscles and bones let you, if you're in your 30s' more of what I said about the 20's but a little easier on your joints, 40 will be at your doorstep sooner than you think. If you're over 40 it's not the end, far from it, remember it's what you think that counts so remember to focus on thinking and then acting on what you can do and not what you can't. It's never too late to start, you just need to decide what it is and start again. Look at Colonel Tom, he decided to do something good and became a national hero at the age of 99. Amazing! Sadly, since I started writing this Captain Sir Tom Moore has passed away at the age of 100 what a truly inspiring person he was. Remember, the only thing you have is time, don't waste it on doing fuck all!

DEATH Chapter 16

The Immortality Project

F.E.A.R. – Ian Brown

'I am not afraid of death, I just don't want to be there when it happens' Woody Allen

While researching this book, with relatively innocuous Google searches I stumbled on a conspiracy site, that had a load of BS in it about governments using our minds against us etc but while I was there I did discover a book that peaked my interest. The book is called The Denial of Death by Ernest Becker where he suggests that everything we do, think and feel is motivated by distracting us from the thought of our death or an attempt to avoid death itself by transcending it through leaving a legacy that lasts after our bodies have given up the ghost (good phrase).

Pretty interesting and if you think about it deep enough, it kind of makes sense. Becker suggests that we all have an awareness that it's not a forever type gig and so we attempt to either distract ourselves from thinking about it or we attempt to create heroic symbols of ourselves while we're here so that we beat death itself by being remembered for what we've done while we're here. He calls these symbols of remembrance 'immortality projects' which serve to leave our mark on the world once we're gone. I guess this book that you're reading would be my immortality project (maybe I should have called the book that).

Anyway, another book that kind of reinforces this view is The Fear of Being Disliked which suggests if we cause a scene, we are subconsciously either trying to bring attention to ourselves to get attention/ sympathy from the 'pack' i.e. other people or we are using it to defend ourselves from attack from an external party thus avoiding death. If we are reclusive, we are avoiding death by not exposing ourselves to the world and others that may cause us danger. All of these activities are obviously subjective to the person undertaking them and almost definitely mostly subconscious. From my view, I appear to be an extrovert however, I wasn't always and probably, if I think about it not a natural one at all, but by being the centre of attention I feel I have a sense of control over the situation and all of the eyes on me. I'm hoping these eyes like me and are there to support and protect me. So, my tactic to avoid death is by making myself a human target, well done me for the most random way to protect myself. If I was about in dinosaur times I would have dressed up like a giant steak to avoid being eaten by a T-Rex. Duh!! Anyways, I don't so I'm lucky as on the whole our society (kind of) appreciates someone who is willing to put themselves up for self-ridicule if not to take the attention and chance of death away from themselves. In dinosaur times the other cavemen would love that I was dressed up as a giant steak because it meant they weren't getting eaten, today at least.

Back to the fear of death stuff, it really resonated with me as I remember when I was a kid one of the biology lessons was talking about why we existed and if my memory serves me correctly it was to procreate. That was it, like the Coronavirus we are just here to multiply and continue our species. Of course, Darwin also covered this off with his book 'Origin of the Species' and his theory of evolution (my eldest destroyed my eardrums a few years back by playing Darwin Rocks soundtrack over and over again). Somewhere along the lines our brain chemistry has got a bit too big for its boots and decided that we're here for a higher purpose than to fuck and get sprogs before we die, like a mayfly that's decided to get a career in banking in its 24-hour lifespan (although to him it seems like a fuck long time I guess). Why have we decided to fill the gap between being born, hunting, shagging and dying? Why have we chosen such inane shit to do, and in some cases not doing the shagging bit because the time fillers and distractors have made you so impotent or unattractive to the opposite species we've lost any chance of achieving the reason for our existence, or maybe it's just that you're an ugly cunt. Sorry just joking, you're not really, I think you're beautiful!

So, at some point we decided that living our own lives was more important than living a life for someone else. If I'm honest I only realised any of this stuff once I had kids. I never really thought I'd have kids as I was too busy doing crazy stuff dressed as a giant steak, getting drunk, dancing on tables, jumping out of windows and sleeping in bushes (you know the usual). But when the first little man came into the world, everything seemed to make sense. I knew why I was here and all of the dogshit in my life got removed fast, and when the second little dude popped out recently, that got even more reinforced. Whenever I speak to anyone now I always say I'm pleased I've had children because those little mites gave me purpose and all the bullshit went out the window to help them survive. This is my view and yours (rightly so) can be a different view. Also, I have to admit when they were born, the first thought on my mind wasn't; I really hope they get a stable job in an office, it was I hope they are fucking awesome little rock stars and I will encourage and support them to do whatever the fuck they want.

My eldest is 8 and I can already see the bullshit piling on from homework and peer pressure and I want to save him from it but also want him to be part of the pack and not a weird outsider. I look back on my life and remember discounting hippies and goths being who they were just being what they wanted to be. They probably discounted me for being a chav with Reebok Classic trainers and an Armani symbol on my nose piercing, yes sadly this is true. Thank god camera phones weren't invented back then!

So, if as a species we have been spoilt and at the same time distracted what can we do about it? Well my view is to not shy away from the fact. We are here once, we have so many days (chances) to follow our dreams and become happy but even that will be fleeting and not prevent death itself. The odd mistake here or there ultimately means nothing. Make sure you have the right immortality project on the go while at the same time acknowledging that that is what it is. Be honest with yourself, your existence, your job, your family, your art, your habits are your hobby while you're alive, you can make them as big and far reaching or small and intricate as you want but ultimately, they are yours and as long as you like it who gives a fucking shit what anyone else thinks. And importantly if you don't like what you're doing remember it's just an immortality project, so you can (and probably) should change it.

DEATH Chapter 17

Look Death in the Fucking Face

Stronger – Kanye West

'Life is what happens while you're busy making other plans' John Lennon

I first got the courage and motivation to start podcasting and launch my last book 'The Money Mistakes of Mom & Dad' when I thought I was genuinely going to die (young). I had thought mistakenly for the second time in my life that I had testicular cancer (due to aching bollocks if you must know, jeez nosey!). Both times it has thankfully turned out to be nothing, but I recommend getting checked just in case, as you never know and for the sake of about 10 minutes total with your crinkly tea bag out in a stranger's hands while he checks 'em it's worth it. Honestly, and this goes for women too, you're better off knowing if something's going on, rather than pretending that nothing's wrong and hoping for the best. Actually, this goes for any lump, bump or ailment you're worried about, get it checked.

Why have I gone on about this so much this is meant to be about something else? Thanks for the lecture detour brain.

Moving on, the reason I managed to launch my podcast and finish my book and get it published (more immortality projects) was because I had the fear of dying in me. If you hadn't worked it out already that's the whole idea of this book, using the thought (perhaps fear) of death to motivate you to do the things you want to be doing before it's too late and you're 6 feet underground in a box or floating in the wind as ash. So, during the discovery phase of said aching balls it was like a massive flashing neon sign came to me saying 'DO NOT WASTE YOUR LIFE BECAUSE YOU'LL SOON BE DEAD' and this kicked my ass into action. Just writing that bit of the sentence in capitals has *just* made me switch back into reality, where I've since fallen back into bad habits of procrastination and fear as I'd forgotten I'm not immortal. Don't worry this happens, it's noticing when it does that is the secret. I'm talking about fear, harnessing the fear of death, and converting it into the fear of the memory of an empty life. Looking right at your own death in the fucking face, remembering it and then using it to make you powerful in the here and now.

But if we don't think about it'll be fine, so it's all ok right? Wrong! Evolutionary theorists such as Darwin and Dawkins suggest that everything we do or don't do is directly or indirectly for the purpose of passing on our genes to the next generation and at the same time avoiding death in order to help this process. My (amateur psychologist) theory is that our lives have become so (relatively) easy and luxurious thanks to modern technology and increased disposable incomes that the thought or fear of death has become so abhorrent to our modern trappings, our minds have taken to avoiding even the thought of death. In doing so we have forgotten what we are on the planet to do; reproduce, help our genes survive and quite possibly have a good time while doing it. Fucked up theory I know, but my suggestion is that we have to strengthen our resolve and acknowledge it, by looking it straight in the eye and sticking our middle fingers up at death himself by one acknowledging that we are alive and then acknowledging that it is not forever. Maybe then we can realise that it is a powerful thing to do, to allow us to appreciate (and maximise) our tiny lives that we've been blessed with.

Say it aloud right now 'I am going to fucking die' again 'I AM GOING TO FUCKING DIE' louder 'I AM GOING TO FUCKING DIE!', probably don't do this if there's kids in the room but when they've gone to bed fill your boots. I know it's scary and I don't really want to die either, but I also don't want to avoid the topic so much that I forget to do stuff while I'm here, waste my life and only realise when it's too late that I should have done something today or tomorrow. There are already bits that it's not possible for me to do like I don't think an Olympic gold medal is on the cards for me but there are plenty of other things that I can do to keep my interest and my life fulfilled and I believe no matter what age you are, you can do the same. Motivated? Me too, let's get to the next chapter!

DEATH Chapter 18

24 Hours to Go

21 Seconds – So Solid Crew

'Do not fear death, only the unlived life' Natalie Babbitt

The title of this chapter instantly makes me think of the So Solid Crew's banger of a tune '21 seconds'. If you have your Alexa data spy machine near give it a listen, it might bring a smile to your face, but then again if you hate rap music like my dad, it may provoke you to wish for a sooner death to the band and/ or yourself. Lol. Anyway, my question is, if you had one day to live what would you do? Seriously. Imagine medical peeps have designed an app that gives you a relatively accurate time for your death, you download it to your iPhone and click the app's icon. You fill in the survey and the loading circle starts going, you look away hoping your demise is a long way off and up it pops 23 hours and 59 minutes. Shit! You're on your last day on earth and the clock is ticking, you do a quick Google to check the accuracy and shit it's 98% so it's highly fucking likely that you won't see much (if any) of tomorrow. Fuck. What are you going to do with this 23 hour and a bit period? Check Facebook? look at cats falling over on YouTube? Go to work? Worry about politics? No, I didn't think so, and why is that? Because those things are (dun dun derrrr) fucking time fillers! Things to do when you think you have got time to spare or even waste. Because when your time is limited the unimportant stuff you've been doing becomes even more unimportant and the important stuff well, that becomes imperative. The quote by Natalie Babbitt at the start of this chapter, has something magical in its simplicity; basically, those that fear death only fear it because they have not lived their life to the fullest, so panic that they have wasted their life or at the very least not maximised any (or much) of their potential.

If you could go back and interview your parents while you were still in the womb about the hopes and dreams that they have for you, you can pretty much guarantee that it wasn't that you live unhappily in a dead-end job, with a barely noticeable existence. They more than likely wanted you to arrive with a bang and live an amazing life with twists, turns and excitement or at least doing what you want to do and not just what pays the bills with someone that you kind of like but treats you like dog turd. YOU HAVE A LIFE, YOU ARE ALIVE. LIVE YOUR LIFE!

If it was me and I was told that I had 24 hours to go I would probably do a quick few minutes on social media to say good bye and then grab my closest family and talk as much as possible with them, hug them for dear life (as long as it wasn't Covid or something contagious I was dying from!) and absorb as much of them as possible. I would do the same if the app said this about any of my close friends and family too.

Why do we wait until the last minute to go and see someone? Yes, it may be comforting for the individual if they're in the hospital but why didn't you go and see them when they were fine? Why weren't you able to find the time or the justification to see them then? Are you there to remind you of what they looked like? Parkinson's Law explains this somewhat as it states that "work expands so as to fill the time available for its completion". Because we assume that we have a load of years ahead of us then we can do all the things that we want to do including seeing our families and following our dreams, at some time in the future when work and lazing about is finished. We all make excuses and procrastinate and assume we'll do the things at a later date, but the sands of time are constantly falling, and you never know what is around the corner, whether it be a car accident, illness or something else. Something that could stop you doing what you've always wanted to. Right I'm quickly off to give my wife and the boys a cuddle, I'm also going to get someone to tune my piano and book piano lessons. God this book is inspiring. Lol. *Note it turns out the piano I've had for eight years was actually broken beyond repair and had to be scrapped. Ha! RIP old friend.

Sadly, or maybe not so sadly, the app doesn't exist, and probably never will. So, we have to assume that it could be any time; today or even tomorrow that is your last chance to experience life. Ask yourself, are you doing enough? Are you maximising your time? Have you followed your dreams? Have you spoken to that old friend or family member you've fallen out with? Do you want to get around to it fucking now?! I have seen family feuds last for years and then the individuals shit themselves when one of them gets ill, what's the fucking point in this? Don't spend your life holding grudges assuming you can make up another time. Grow the fuck up and be the bigger person before it's too late! They're probably wishing they could speak to you too and if they're not then fuck them but at least you tried goddamit!

DEATH Chapter 19

Let's Talk about Death Baby

Talk Tonight – Oasis

'Just fucking talk about death' Adam Jones (Me)

Part of the reason we don't think about death is because we don't talk about it. My view is that death (like sex) has become a thing of movie fantasy and is not often discussed unless someone is about to or has actually died, even then the topic is brushed over until you're drunk at the wake. It is suggested that the fear of death can be attributed to a number of psychological disorders from panic attacks to compulsive checking. Other (in some cases unhealthy) habits have also been suggested to fuel our avoidance of death such as drinking alcohol, watching excessive amounts of TV and shopping to name but a few. Wow who'd have thought me getting pissed and watching TV all night was about death? Not me I can tell you that for free. But if you think about it, it perversely kind of makes sense, what else could I be shutting out and filling my brain and body with shit for? Fucked up man!

Is it because of the mystery of what happens that has made it such a taboo or is that because no one has a definitive answer no one wants to put their thoughts forward? I mentioned earlier in the book that I thought about death a lot when I was younger, and I remember it being swept under the carpet as soon as I'd broach the topic of either me or my family dying. When I was told that my nan, that I had spent a lot of my early years with, had cancer I remember running to my room and then my parents distracting me away from the thought of it. The only time we acknowledged it was at the wake and even then, I was too young to understand. Years later when you're an adult it kind of gets dealt with but by then it's too late and the social taboo is already formed.

I've done the same to my boy when his hamster Katie passed away, I gave him some magical chat about being in the stars, but the truth was I didn't know where she'd gone. I understand that it's not a palatable topic for an 8-year-old and I get my parents didn't want to deal with my sleepless nights when they told me we get put into a box and either burnt or buried and that was the end of our existence forever.

I witnessed real life dead people (grandparents), I went to funerals, but no one seemed to talk about it except in the religious sense of the word. 'They've gone to heaven' or 'they're watching over you' and it wasn't until GCSE science 3 or 4 years later that the topic was actually talked about scientifically, you know the need for breathing and heart pumping blood and shit. But there's still a piece of the jigsaw missing in my view the spiritual side, the fact that we have a soul and personality, where does that go does it disappear along with our body and is it just unique to this set of skin and bones or does it go elsewhere into the atmosphere?

My belief is that as many of us have moved away from a traditional religion which prescribed an afterlife and heaven, we've stopped acknowledging it happens at all. I think we need to not only think about death more but talk about it with our friends, families especially our children. Not in a morbid way (if we can help it) but in a 'ooh what do you think happens' kind of way. A curiosity as to what it feels like and what happens once it's happened in a none judgmental way in order to make it less of a cultural taboo, bizarrely as I'm writing this I have just seen a section on this on Steph's Packed Lunch on Channel 4. Cool! Also, while researching this topic I have discovered that there are some clever people that have thought the same (I wasn't so arrogant to think I was the first honest!). Karen Van Dyke based in San Diego has created something called 'Death Cafes' where people can go and have open conversations about death and what it means to them. What a great idea? But this can also start at home with your family. As they've got older I have discussed with my mom and dad about their feelings about death (I think with my mom on one of my first podcasts) as well as being much more open with my son than they were with me, I can see him getting sad about it, so I don't push too hard.

The key message is to remove the stigma of talking about death so it's less of a shock for you and your loved ones when someone you know dies or you have an illness. This will also help to stop unhealthy thoughts and conversations taking place in secret. Make death part of our conversations (we all have it in common) and take some ownership back from action movies where the goody kills a henchman and just moves on to the next one without a second thought for that man's friends and family, although this was acknowledged in

Austin Powers movies. Life and death should be talked about equally, it doesn't stop it happening by ignoring it.

DEATH Chapter 20

Imagine Your Funeral

Play Dead – Bjork

'As is a tale so is life: Not how long it is but how good
it is, is what matters' Seneca

Have you ever walked through a crematorium grounds
or a grave yard and looked at the older head stones and
memorials? I have, mainly because I've always lived
quite close to them and when I do, I always try to work
out the ages of the people that are buried there and then
how long it has been since they've passed compared
to when they died. I also look to see how recent the
flowers and cards are. I'm not being morbid (or maybe
I am) but this knowledge makes me think about their
families and if they are still remembered now. I think
about the fact that their relatives had felt enough about
them to bury them with a headstone for people to visit
and be remembered by, or perhaps they arranged it
themselves, who the fuck knows? But it also makes

me think about my own funeral, when and where I'll finally rest. I will be cremated so I won't be lying in the ground being eaten by worms, but I will have some kind of service and it's what will be said at this service about me that intrigues me the most.

I am hoping to have a lot of people there that I have impacted in a positive way (maybe even you?), I hope I am referred to as an author and musician rather than an office worker, I hope I have helped a number of people and they remember this fact enough to pay their last respects to me and I want to leave a legacy of financial security for my loved ones. This is my list of stuff, yours might be entirely different, you may be wanting to be seen for the people you've taught or sporting achievements or something else completely random and unique to you e.g. best pork pie jelly creator. This is good because we are all different and all have different desires for how our lives turn out. However, if we come back to now, I am still (at the time of writing) an office worker, I try to help people, I have set up life insurance and got a pension ready for my wife and kids, I am writing this book and still in a band. I am in most part (apart from the office job) aiming towards my funeral goal (ok so that really does sound fucking morbid!) and my question is are you heading towards your desired end? If you are then great, if not why not? And how can you start to do so?

Don't worry I find that most people I speak to, don't contemplate that they are going to die and definitely don't think about their funeral except for (oddly) the song that they want playing. I want 'Live Forever' by Oasis by the way. But this lack of thought about the end means a lot of people seem to be living day to day, stumbling into jobs and relationships without any thought of the long-term outcomes of those (seemingly) insignificant decisions and life choices. Funnily enough,

I've just remembered a song with my first ever band and it was called Falling Through Life about this very topic. Back then I didn't know how much I was on to something until now.

Think about what was said about you as a kid; he/ she is smart, he/ she is athletic, he/ she will go far. Think about your talents hidden or otherwise, think about your passions and your interests. What did you love to do? What did you spend all of your time doing? Now what is your job? What does your spare time look like? Is it drinking/ drugs and watching TV? Are you following your calling? Based on your life at the moment what will be said at your funeral? Is it what you want to be said because if it isn't, it's time to fucking change shit up right now. Don't get me wrong if you want to be known as the greatest drinker ever that's fine and Oliver Reed (one of my heroes) was known for this. I'm saying if the things that you are doing do not fit what you want for your future, you have to reflect and wake up now, starting today start to change the things that don't fit and start to add in the things that do.

It is never too late to start again as long as you still have a fucking breath in your lungs. Yes, it might take you a little while to catch up and you may never be the top of the game depending on your age, but you can have a bloody good go and remember the world loves a trier and the best time to start anything is right now. Make your goals and desires your habit, make your interests and hobbies your life and make your future self be proud of yourself now, because if you do one day (before you die) you will look back and feel good about what you've achieved, even if you started late or had a blip in the middle. As soon as you make a start doing what you want to do you will notice a difference in all aspects of your life. In the words of Nike; Just Fucking Do It. *Note they don't say Fucking.

DEATH Chapter 21

Everyone You Know Someday Will Die

Holocene – Bon Iver

'How can the dead be truly dead when they live in the souls of those who are left behind?' Carson McCullers

In this book so far, we've covered your death but only partly touched on other people's. I'm afraid to say that everyone you know today will at some point die. I know it's obvious, but I think sometimes we lull ourselves into a fantasy that our loved ones will live forever. This fantasy is kind of ok however, while believing this fact we may tend to take them for granted. They were here today so it's only logical that they'll be here tomorrow, well one day that logic will be disproved. They will be there one day and either you or them will not be there the next and this fucking sucks big time (unless you didn't like them!). Having lost all of my grandparents, an uncle, a great uncle, my best friend's mom and a couple more family friends, I can tell you 'fucking sucks' doesn't quite contain the pain that this departure brings. It's also amplified by the deafening silence of people not wanting to talk about their death or in fact them as a person, for quite some time after (except of course when they're drunk at the funeral because magically it's allowed then!). As a child of eleven when my nan passed away I didn't really see her much just before she died, I get that my parents thought it might be too upsetting for me as we were really close, but the lack of visibility increased the feeling of macabre for me, instead of letting me see her become frail, they hid her away to 'protect' me from witnessing the inevitable of someone that I held so dear.

I honestly can't say what I would have done if I were them. Cancer is a fucking cunt of a thing and perhaps my relatively naïve eyes would have been disturbed, but surely the hiding it from me would have heightened my imagination to fill in the gaps which was probably worse than the thing itself.

I am assuming that you are older than eleven and the bad news is that the loss is still a motherfucker like a pickaxe through a water pipe, it leaves you feeling empty and drained. What I will say is that if you have spent lots of time with the person that has passed this empty feeling is eventually filled back up with warm fluffy feelings of memories that pop into your head when you hear a song or remember something about them. I was only eleven (so 30 years ago) I still remember my nan's favourite song and the feeling of being wrapped up in her cardigan (smelling of cigarettes and lavender) for a cuddle. Mad really, when I can barely remember what I had for dinner yesterday!

So how do we avoid regretting someone's passing? *Note that I did not say avoid feeling sad. There is a simple answer; make sure you dedicate enough time to that person to feel that you truly experienced who they were to you. Give them the best gift you can give them; a PS5! No, your time, let them know that you love them and expect nothing in return. As long as you've made the effort while they are alive you will have nothing to regret when they pass. If you forget them when they're alive, this will be where the regret comes from. Also, if you are holding a grudge against someone and they are still alive, if they didn't kill or abuse someone to cause the grudge, phone them up today and try to make amends. Fuck your pride, talk to them, go and see them, tell them that you love them. If you're struggling, imagine if the next phone call that you have is that they have died. How does that feel? Do you wish you'd spoken to them? In the words of Jordan Beaufort; 'pick up the phone and keep dialling'. Yes, a quote that has nothing to do with the topic but who cares? Phone your loved ones tell them that you love them, tell them how shit that quote was if you have to but don't leave it too late, as they'll be dead forever and you won't be able to fix anything then.

As for the loved ones that pass that you did have a good relationship with and did spend enough time with what about them? It still bloody hurts, possibly more as they're missing from your life after being such a big part. Make sure you watch the Pixar film Coco (be warned it's a bit of a tear jerker!), this teaches you the very basic principles of the day of the dead in Mexico but essentially says that the living keeps their family alive in the afterlife by remembering them on that particular day by displaying their photograph and lighting a candle for them. My view is that this is good but do it more often than just one day. Talk about them, celebrate their birthday, have their favourite tipple and look at photographs and videos of them. Yes, sometimes it will make you sad but sometimes it will make you happy that you remembered them and regardless of whether there is an afterlife or not it will help you remember that you and your surviving relatives are mortal. Avoiding pain is only a temporary fix, the more you can acknowledge and live with it the stronger you become and the less painful it will seem. Don't shy away from pain in your mind as it will only come out at a later date; like me crying about a ginger kid singing for his nan on the Tonight's the Night with John Barrowman after not crying at my own nan's funeral, which is a true story ha!

DEATH Chapter 22

Don't Kill Yourself (Keep Turning Up)

Cycle of Hurt – Doves

'The bravest thing I ever did was continuing my life when I wanted to die' Juliette Lewis

I have felt properly suicidal twice in my life, times where I was so low that the very thought of carrying on with the pain of what was happening was worse than the prospect of not existing on the planet. Apart from the events that had triggered these feelings there were other factors at play, excessive alcohol consumption, gambling addiction and lack of sleep primarily from the two just mentioned. This cyclical mistreatment of myself had led my brain from a relatively joyous young chap to a miserable fucker in a matter of months, I'm being flippant sorry, I was depressed. Luckily for me, I had a strong best friend and family network and I had

had the added bonus of doing psychology at A-level and realised (even in a rudimentary way) that there may be other factors at play and indeed another route.

I was also lucky enough to live in a generation where it was quite acceptable for a man to admit he had emotional problems and a counsellor wasn't seen as a sign of 'going mental'. Now I am not saying the things that happened to me are any worse or better than the things that may cause you or someone you know to want to kill yourself, but I do believe problems in their purest sense are all relative. As in I believe that any problem could be detrimental to your health and wellbeing given enough shit already endured and a little dodgy brain chemistry coming in to play. However, what I am saying is that no matter how bad you feel right now life can get better. Time heals all wounds as they say and if I could have told myself at the time I wanted to kill myself that in 5 years' time I would be happier than I had ever been I would have never believed myself but here I am. And there lies the problem, the feeling like shit feeling makes you continue to feel like shit and then cruelly, make you analyse why you can't stop thinking and why you feel shit and the cycle of sadness continues. If you can stop thinking about it through counselling, prescription drugs, meditation or Cognitive Behavioural Therapy (CBT) it can interrupt the cycle of hurt which incidentally is the excellent song I have included for this chapter.

You may think I am lucky and maybe I am, your brain will automatically assume I've had it easier than you and I haven't experienced the pain or hardship that you have, but assuming that you've got it worse than everyone else can only get you so far in life (you may have I don't know). If you're truthful with yourself, you can probably imagine someone worse off than you. If you can't, skip straight to the suicide hotline at the end of this chapter.

As a child when I first learnt what suicide was I couldn't quite comprehend why people didn't just leave the situation or move towns to get away from whatever was causing them pain. It was only later on in life, as an adult that I realised that it's not the situation or physical location that is the problem it is inside your head where the true damage is done. No matter where you go, your brain is still there, talking shit to you, making you feel like utter dog crap. This was pretty much my life for a good while until I read an excellent book called the Chimp Paradox by Dr. Steve Peters. I'd heard of the book on a breakfast chat show where Peters talked of working with people like Ronnie O'Sullivan, whom I also was and still am a fan of. I thought if this worked for Ronnie it could work for me. I won't go into the theory of the book (I want you to read it for yourself) but the main thing I gained from it was that by attempting to stop the terrible thoughts and feelings through things by distraction (alcohol, drugs, gambling, sex etc) or solving (meditation, positive thinking, counselling) or just trying to avoid them completely and not acknowledging them because they are too painful was actually keeping the thoughts 'alive' in my brain, making the problem worse.

Dr. Peters encourages you to just acknowledge the thought, let it out, using the books terminology giving your inner chimp the voice until he gets knackered and then normal thinking can return. This was a game changer for me as by letting out all of the bullshit thoughts even encouraging some of them and expanding on them until the (sometimes dark) topics were over, I could then get to sleep or concentrate on my job or do whatever I needed to without the monkey on my back (excuse the pun).

So, if you do find yourself in a repetitive negative/ dark thinking loop like I was. Don't try to stop the thoughts, let them happen. Give them airtime and remember that

that is all they are; just thoughts, they are not you, once you've had a good old think about them, move on, the fighting against them makes them more likely to occupy your mind whereas the acknowledging and moving on lets them go. Another tip I have learnt along the way is to also, give yourself a time slot to think about the shit things. If you are attempting to do your job but getting distracted about a recent break up or piece of bad news, say to your brain (internally) 'thanks for bringing this to my attention, if you don't mind I'm quite busy right now, can I think about this at say 9pm tonight when I've done what I need to do'. My brain usually lets me do this and by the time 9pm comes I've usually forgot about what it was I was thinking.

Whatever you are feeling, suicide is not the answer, all it does is cause pain and heartache for the ones that you leave behind that you probably love and love you too. No matter how worthless you feel, no matter what you've done I can almost guarantee that you still mean something to someone and your life is precious. I know the feeling, where you just feel the world will be better off without you but fuck that. Be brave, be stubborn keep fucking living and stick your two fingers up at the world and death and prove that you are worth more. If you don't like your situation change it, but don't die as it's too final and there's no coming back and there's so much you can still do. DO NOT KILL YOURSELF. Talk to a friend or member of your family. If you are feeling suicidal and can't confide in anyone close, please contact the Samaritans on 116-123, talking to someone will help.

SECTION 2

LIVING & DYING

LIVING Chapter 23

You Are Going to Fucking Live

Live Forever – Oasis

'Your eyes look within. Are you satisfied with the life you are living?' Bob Marley

Despite this book being designed to remind you of your own mortality, I also want to make it crystal clear that you are not dying yet. Yes, you are going to fucking die, but you are also going to fucking live. You, me, while we're here, we have an opportunity to have a wonderful time, but I think somewhere during the crossover from childhood to adulthood (puberty, exams, jobs etc) we forget this fact. Life can be about having a good time and doesn't have to be about just working, worrying and complaining, unless you like doing these things then in that case fill your boots and forget everything that I've said so far. It's almost like guilt is perversely linked to our happiness; we can't feel happy because of other bad stuff in the world but we can't live in a constant state of worry and dismay no matter how bad things are either. I believe we should actively seek out joy, despite shit going on elsewhere potentially in our own lives, families or locations. Obviously, I'm not saying piss yourself laughing while visiting someone in the hospital (well unless they are too) but what I am saying is try to see some light, as I feel we have been blessed with a sense of humour and a smile to use as well as the sad faces and tears.

You can worry and turn everything into a disaster but as Corrie Ten Boom states 'Worry does not empty tomorrow of its sorrow; it empties today of its strength'. If you think about it honestly anything you've worried about in your life has probably either not come true, not been as bad as you were expecting or even if it was then you've eventually recovered from it. If you're not there yet, don't worry you will. See that's the beauty of life, the more you keep waking up, eating, sleeping and living, and doing other shit the more we forget the painful things and the more we attract better things and even if they're not necessarily better they are different. It may not be instantly, sometimes we need to go through a grieving process but sometimes it can happen pretty quickly. What's that old phrase? As god closes a door he opens a window.

I have been heartbroken in my life, I mean shit stuff on top of bollocks with a side order of crap fries happened to me in my 30's and if I think back to the pinnacle of my pain, I felt like I would never know happiness again, but guess what? I kept turning up, punching the clock, doing the time, feeling the pain and then one day, I didn't think about that pain or those people anymore. Don't get me wrong it hasn't disappeared from my mind completely, occasionally it sneaks up and gives me a kick in the bellend moment of 'ah shit' but then I continue in my life now which is happy and sorted and I move on. I know that if I continued to think about the people or events it would take me back down there where I was, but the choice I have is not to think about it, and this stops me from experiencing it over and over again. This can happen for you, as long as you want it to.

My theory is that some people have had so much shit go on that the pain is now a normal (almost comfortable) place rather than a shit space to be in. This painful comfort means that you stay down there for too long but perversely means more shit is likely to come your way. The thing (or things) that happened, happened during a particularly influential or poignant time in your life and led you to wallow for just a bit too long. I had a period of about 5 years where it was one thing after another and looking back it was a cumulative effect of shite happening to me, I didn't deal with anything very well, so more stuff kept coming and if I'm being so honest that it hurts me to write, I quite possibly enjoyed the role of the victim. Ahh that stings to say, but yes, the attention and sympathy may have been comforting for me, so didn't object to it either. Thank fuck I snapped out of that shit show.

This will sound very harsh (and somewhat implausible) but happiness is a choice. Right now, no matter how crap you're feeling I just want you to force a smile and count for 10 seconds. Even if you don't want to and feel it's stupid please do it, guess why? Because a University of Tennessee 2019 study found that smiling makes us feel better. Wow! Yes, it's true, the thing that we do because we are happy can also be the cause of making us happier too. Now I'm not naïve to think forcing a smile solves every problem but the more you do anything over and over can make small differences to your wellbeing. My tip is when you notice yourself thinking about the thing that has happened, distract yourself, think of other things, meditate, get a hobby, speak to someone (but not about the thing), go for a walk, anything just to avoid it entering your consciousness. If it is persistent then clear half an hour from your schedule to Chimp Paradox it and let your brain let rip, I mean swear and scream (internally) at it, agree with it, let it say the hurtful things and go for it, and when it's finished, leave it there, lying knackered on the floor and say to it 'don't bother me for a fucking month, I got shit to do'.

LIVING Chapter 24

Excuses, Excuses

Little Lion Man – Mumford and Sons

'If it's important to you, you will find a way. If not, you'll find an excuse' Daniel Decker

What is an excuse? You may smile but I mean really, what are they? Reasons for doing or not doing something. But why do you need a reason to do or not to do something? It's your life you don't HAVE to do anything if you don't want to, but day in and day out people make up fictitious or spurious reasons to do or avoid doing things. Fuck that! What's the point, my dog ate my homework, did it? No, I just didn't feel like doing it and the schooling system is outdated and only teaches what everyone else in my class knows so what good is that in a world of diversification and individualisation? I forgot my kit to do yoga with you tonight. Did you? No, I just couldn't be arsed to get my clothes off in a cold school hall to put another tighter and frankly more embarrassing outfit on to rub myself across the floor like a fucking sloth, soz. My point that I'm going through great pains to get across is that in a logical world there should be no need to lie or make an excuse. If you have to make an excuse for something, then there's something wrong with your situation and/ or your relationships. I should caveat this with that you could face consequences for doing or not doing the thing, you need to be prepared that by telling the truth you may get in to trouble or at least disappoint someone. Both of these are fine I just want you to be ready for these potential outcomes.

During lockdown, my son told me he didn't want to do Joe Wicks with me, I was absolutely gutted and a little internally angry, why? I'm not a fitness kind of guy and it's only a small thing. If I'm honest it's because my relationship with him was changing and he wasn't as easily influenced by me anymore. Noooooooooo! What happened to my little mate who I could get to do anything with me? Now, I could have shouted and made him do it which could have forced him to make an excuse such as he was hurting from the day before, or he could have reluctantly done it with me. Either of those options would have been pretty shit for both of us, resentment on his part if he'd done it or mistrust on my part if I didn't believe his excuse. Instead I just bargained with him and he agreed that I didn't have to play one of his games that I don't like so bit of a result. Did I do the right thing? I'm not sure, it's hard being a parent, but it does show the origin of where an excuse could have been generated unnecessarily. I always ALWAYS give the actual reason I can or can't do something, and I expect to be treated the same. I have a friend who always uses shit see through excuses and wonder what he thinks I'm going to say if he told me the truth. I have to be honest I'd prefer him to tell the real reason as it would show a certain level of respect for me to handle why I was being stood up etc. Also, it would mean that I could trust him more as part of me thinks if he can lie about something as menial as why he can't come out, what else could he lie to me about? I'm more hurt by the lie to try and not offend me than I would be if he simply told me the truth.

Ask yourself, if you tell the truth or do you make excuses for things? Do you think that everyone totally believes your excuses? What about if they know that they're excuses, and they feel about you like I feel about by friend above? If you think maybe they do and you're not committing any crimes my advice is to start to come clean, I don't mean confess to all your past lies, I mean just start to give the actual reason and see what happens. If I were a betting man (which I have been in the past) I suspect that nothing will change between you. If you don't fancy going out, say to your friends politely, 'I don't fancy it tonight'. If you're not seeing your girlfriend or boyfriend because you're seeing a friend just say 'I have plans'. If you have a secret addiction to Loose Women reruns, well then I probably wouldn't admit to that but just say that you're washing your hair, as a bald man, this is my favourite reason to give for not doing something.

If they love you and respect you, they will respect your reasoning and accept it. Equally, if you do something wrong that causes an accident don't try to shift the blame, take responsibility because in the long run the truth will come out and even if it doesn't you still know the truth and you have to live with the lie, and also you have to remember to lie about it forever. I am a shit liar, mainly because I have a rubbish lying face (I've been told) and I have a terrible memory. Times where I have lied I have ended up blurting it out just because my conscience couldn't deal with it. I instantly felt better once I did. Set yourself free by telling the truth, forget excuses, be brave and I reckon you will feel better and probably have stronger relationships with those around you in the long run.

LIVING Chapter 25

How to Get Shit Done

Get Busy – Sean Paul

'Doing things is not the same as getting things done'
Jared Silver

This chapter, which I wasn't expecting to write is a result of me starting to write the last bit of that last chapter and realising that for me it's easy to do more than the norm (i.e. extra shit). I had and thankfully have two loving parents that said I could do or be anything I wanted except sing in a band and guess what I fucking showed them by being the lead singer of a band for the last 25 years. In your face Ha! Anyways they were really supportive and gave me a lot of confidence, but your folks, upbringing, background, friends, lifestyle, personality might not have blessed you with the self-confidence that I have. Wait scratch that, I haven't got self-confidence, I've just chosen wisely which fucks I give and if what I attempt fails I have the ability to laugh about it. So, I thought I'd pop this mini chapter in to see if it helps you get the things you want to do done – there I go thinking again but I don't give a fuck if it's different or goes wrong so here goes nothing.

Step 1. What is it that you would love to do? I mean really, close your eyes and imagine what you would do if there were no barriers and no judgments, what would you be doing with your life? What would make you leap out of bed, don't say a boring office job! But seriously, what have you always wanted to do but always been afraid of people taking the piss out of, not having enough money, not having the right talent, not having the right appearance. Just blurt it out, if you're on the train just say it in your head. Once you have it move to Step 2.

Step 2. What is it that is stopping you do it? Ok I want you to list the things that are holding you back from being what you want to be. Get a piece of paper, write the thing you want to do at the top and write down everything that you see as a barrier. For example, if you want to be a mermaid, your first barrier could be 'I can't fucking swim' or if you want to be a race car driver it could be 'I can't drive'. These blockers can be perceived or real I just want you to do the exercise of seeing what is actually stopping you following your ultimate passion or goal. Once you have created your list, move on to Step 3.

Step 3. Get another piece of paper and move all of the facts from the first list to the new piece of paper. E.g. You do need to be able to drive to be a racing driver so move that, if you said I'm too old that's opinion so leave that on the old list. Once complete, go to the toilet, have a shit and wipe your ass with the first list. Do you know why I'm saying this? Because these barriers are in your head (clue from chapter 1, you're thinking them). You have been told by other folks or decided from watching or reading something that you can't do something because of X reason. Well that's hopefully now covered in brown poop down your toilet. These are lies to programme you to forget your dreams (immortality project) and join the drudgery of the rat race. You are not a rat so why race them? People no, fuck it, we ALL look at someone else doing something and wish that we could do it, we all look at other people embarking on something and have a hint of jealousy and if they ask our opinion may sew the seed of doubt for them. Well people do the same to us. If someone says to you it's too hard to do something that's because they're scared to do it and even more scared that you might do it instead of them. If Richard Branson or Bill Gates listened to all the folks telling them they'd fail we wouldn't have Virgin or Microsoft. I have told my little lad he can be anything that he wants and if he fails it's a good thing because it means he can learn and improve until he can do it.

Step 4. What would be the smallest step you could take to get started? Right, time for serious (small) action and please before starting this make sure you've flushed your list before you get shit everywhere. Ever heard the cliché, every long journey starts with the first step, well it's true isn't it? You can't skip the first step, you'd fall over and even if you jumped over where the first step was that would just turn that into the first step wouldn't it? Without the first step your trip doesn't start. Take the new list, you have the blockers on the left side of the paper and now start thinking of what you can do to overcome them and write those on the right-hand side. If you need money, you can ask friends to lend it you, or maybe a bank. If you're unfit and you want to be a runner, write down how you can start to get fit, e.g. take the stairs and don't get the escalator. Once you've got all these down, rank the tasks to achieve them from the simplest thing to do at the top and the hardest to do at the bottom. Then do the simplest task, and this might be something like, if you want to be a runner

'Google running clubs in my local area', whoa pretty easy yes but you're thinking life should be hard to get a reward shouldn't it? No, not with my method, I want you to build momentum slowly, Richard Branson didn't start off by taking on a massive airline, he started by selling pencils and stuff outside his Uni to make cash. You have to begin somewhere and the easiest one to do will reward your brain enough to get you interested in doing the next simplest activity. Slowly slowly catchy monkey when it comes to motivation and eventually the momentum will build. Sticking with the same example the next task might be 'email the running clubs to see if they have any availability', no commitment there but you've made another step towards being a runner. You've started a conversation, but you're tricking your brain to making an effort and having small rewards each time you move forward.

Now as these tasks go on and get harder you will come across difficulties and you may not succeed in all of the tasks first time but keep at it. You should expect to fail, and this might make you feel disheartened. Other people may be willing you to fail so they don't have to be better than they are and motivate themselves away from watching dross like Love Island like you are. I tell my lad it's ok to fail, as you can't grow without failure. I also tell him that when he's bleeding from falling over that blood is a good sign as it means he's alive. Am I lying? Nope.

Back to you, you have to ignore people when you tell them about your plans, or if it's someone who takes the piss and they get to you then you need to keep it to yourself if at all possible until you're doing it and realising you can do it and could've done it all along. You must believe that if it is your passion it is worth fighting for and if you don't do it you are wasting your precious time here on the Covid infected earth. Fuck them, Fuck everyone else you got this, just take that first step! No procrastination no excuse. What's your first step? Grab a beer, put your feet up and turn on the TV or put the beer back, get on Google and make a bloody start?!

LIVING Chapter 26

Fuck Other People

Bulletproof – La Roux

'Be yourself. Everyone else is already taken'
Oscar Wilde

Fuck other people. No not literally, this is not a chapter telling you to cheat on your partner you dirty minded git! I am advocating that you should do most of the things you want to do without worrying about what other people think, so just go for it! But please PLEASE don't do it if it hurts someone else (mentally or physically) or is illegal obviously. I have put this chapter in to tell you the great news; that other people's opinions of you do not need to affect you (and a reminder that your opinions don't have to be taken on board by others either). Firstly, let me qualify that, I am not advocating not caring about other people's feelings or wellbeing and being a selfish asshole, that's reserved just for me (snigger). What I am promoting is doing whatever the fuck you want to do while simultaneously being respectful and not knowingly physically or mentally harming any other human or animal or breaking the law of the country you're in. I'll also say keep your moral compass as well when in countries that are not your own, just because you can doesn't mean that you should.

While you're doing what you want to do, what other people think about you doesn't matter two shits, or even one shit for that matter because their thoughts about it are just that; their thoughts. Wear what you fucking want, dance as shit as you do, say stupid shit because in the end it doesn't really matter. Robin Sharmer and a few other people have said that 'other people's opinions of you are none of your business' and if you think about that statement it's so true. Why do we give so much of a toss about what other people think? And why do we feel the need to change someone else's thoughts about a matter either. Chill. Your thoughts are your thoughts based on your upbringing, experiences and intelligence and theirs are theirs and are based on the different shit that they've been through.

If you disagree with me about what you read in this book then fair enough, but you don't need to email me and tell me because these are my beliefs and you have yours. Stop wasting your life being offended and trying to win arguments and proving that you are right and someone else is wrong. Life is like golf; the only person you're playing against is yourself. Because at your funeral they're not going to say, here lies <insert your name> so much righter about random stuff than <insert your friends name>, why because it doesn't matter who was right or wrong, chances are you both were! Even the genius Stephen Fry did an episode of QI that showed what had been disproved on that show since it aired years before. No one is ever really right or really wrong because none of us know jack shit it is just opinion. Really.

This importance of other people's opinions more than likely starts when we are kids, we realise that good things happened when we behaved a certain way, and that not so good or even bad things happened when were another way. True to Pavlov's theory of 'classical conditioning' like dogs salivating when seeing food and then hearing a bell, and eventually salivating to just the bell without the food. We as little animals started behaving in the way that rewarded us more often and eventually did it without the reward or punishment being there and carried on in to our adult lives where we have less danger around us such as adults telling us off or whatever. *Note the cunts in the world were given the wrong reward and/ or support for the wrong behaviour and that's why they're like that and their kids will probably grow up to be cunts too (they are out there so be warned). Saint Francis Xavier said, 'give me the boy until he is seven and I'll give you the man', meaning that you can influence how kids will grow up to be until a certain age and after that it's a struggle as they're solidified into who they're going to be. Who did you solidify in to? Do you like the person that you are? Good to ask yourself this every now and then.

Remember, Rob Moore states that you are the sum of all of the people that you spend your time with, if you think your friends are twats then I'm sorry to say other people probably think you are a twat too. If you don't like the things that your friends do or say why are they your friends? You can stop seeing them, you can move away, you can change your number, you can even emigrate to find a better group of people to associate yourself with if you're that desperate for change. You probably don't because their opinion of you matters to you and you're trapped, well I'm here to say 'fuck other people' it doesn't matter what they think of you, remember you've only got so many days left do you want to waste it with these losers or do you want to do some cool shit with some truly nice people. I had a period of time where I was in some negative relationships to the point where I thought all girls were knobs, and settled for quite mentally abusive girls, it took me meeting some 'normal' girls to realise I was attracting this behaviour by being desperate to be in a relationship, lowering my self-worth and accepting things that I wouldn't accept today. As soon as this occurred to me I was able to move away and find my wife and settle down. You can do this too. You don't have to settle for shit. Promise.

A year or two ago, I saw Gary Vee at a conference, and he was talking about building an online personal brand and why most people suffer with negative comments from trolls. He basically said, most people value the likes and the complements so much that when a negative comment arrives it makes us crumble. He suggests that we should accept all opinions with the same level of importance and if someone says something that is passed your threshold just reply with a simple phrase 'go fuck yourself' which I think is beautifully eloquent and to the point. It may be tough to fight against years of hardwiring to ignore the opinion of others but try it you might like it.

The real moral of this chapter is to take a stoical approach to life. Don't be too pleased or too disappointed with what comes your way just be accepting of it without extreme reactions either way. We have no clue which direction our lives will take based on the decisions we make, it's chance so it's best to be thankful and continue forward without much judgment on the consequence. Well that was a refreshingly calm conclusion to a chapter I think. Better get in a couple of fuck or buggers to finish it off.

LIVING Chapter 27

Saying Yes to Success (Cheesy Bastard!)

Yes – McAlmont and Butler

'I was saying yes because when you're in love, the
world is full of possibilities, and when you're in love,
you want to take every single one of them'
Danny Wallace

Ooh I love a bit of cheesiness occasionally, don't you?
When you're down often people tell you to think positive
thoughts and even when you're not down people herald
the power of having a positive rather than a negative
outlook to have a better life. And I agree somewhat with
this notion, my advice (even in this book) is that the
more upbeat you frame something that happens the
better it will appear to be. But it can't just be about
your thoughts, otherwise everyone who thinks they're
gonna be a movie star or win the lottery would have, in

my opinion there are another two parts to this puzzle; action and repetition. Just thinking positively about a diagnosis of a life-threatening disease won't cure you, you have to eat healthier, exercise, take the prescribed drugs to help you get better but even then, some shit genetics or some random person could fuck you up.

My mom's uncle Bill was a jolly chap, I loved seeing him as he'd always give me a pound coin and tell rude jokes to my family that I didn't get but I enjoyed seeing him bring laughter and joy to everyone. Anyway, later in his life, he became ill and had gangrene at least I think it was that. He got taken into hospital and they had to remove one of his legs because of the illness. But here's the kicker (poor choice of words!), they didn't tell Bill they had removed it, and when we went to visit we had to not mention it. It was a bizarre situation us all their chatting to Bill with that elephant in the room. We said our good byes and off we left, he seemed his normal self (minus a leg) and thought nothing of it. The next day we got a call, Uncle Bill as he was known to pretty much everyone I know despite probably not being everyone's uncle had passed away. What the fuck?! I thought. How the fuck can this go down? Afterall, he was well when we saw him yesterday! It turned out a porter had arrived at Bill's bed without knowing to keep shtum and said chirpily and I might add innocently to Bill 'how long have you had your leg off'? Bill went into shock and he died. Yes, the disease in his body didn't kill him, a simple, innocently said sentence killed him. Do I use a 'death sentence' joke? Well I did but I loved Uncle Bill and I know he'd have used it himself in one of his anecdotes if he were alive.

Where was I?! Ah yes success, you can't magic cash and success to you by sheer will alone, you have to act i.e. take some action to get there, while thinking positively about getting there and framing what most would see as a negative or a knock back as an opportunity or a driver to continue and kick your goal's proverbial ass cheek! Some years ago, I read Danny Wallace's book Yes Man, his books are enjoyable because they're funny and upbeat but this one in particular struck a chord with me. I'd always been a positive(ish) person but in this book realising his life was drifting into oblivion; in a bid to change things up, Danny attempted to say yes to every question or invite posed to him either by another person or advertisement. This led to some crazy stuff going down with him winning and subsequently losing a cash prize in a newspaper competition and attending parties and getting unexpected job offers all by being positive and saying yes. Now I'm not saying do what Danny did and say yes to everything and anything but what I am saying is that by being open to new opportunities and experiences you will increase the chance of something positive happening to you. Like in my previous book about money; if you say 'no I don't have any change' to the local homeless guy then your brain and the universe thinks you haven't got any change AT ALL, and then works to make that narrative be reality.

If you say no to things, then guess what? Your brain thinks you don't want new, interesting and potentially positive things happening to you, so it doesn't provide these opportunities to you on a regular basis when you might actually want or need them. For instance, how many times has a random unplanned night turned out to be awesome where a pre-planned night you've been looking forward to turns out to be dogshit? You said yes to the random offer of a Wednesday school night drink and your life filled in the gaps with positivity and without a load of planning going into it and it turned out bonza! Don't know where that word came from either but hey, I said yes to it so I'm leaving it in. I ain't arguing with messages from the Australian surf gods in my brain.

I hope you've picked up the moral of the story. It is that, you, yes you, have had lots of things programmed into your brain by the other people knocking about on this planet and some of these people are fucking twats, however the problem with learning from twats is that you may not have known or realised that they are/ were twats. And the bit I really REALLY need you to get is that you don't have to own what they have told you and what they think of you and you also don't have to own what you (and your pesky thoughts) have given you either.

If you feel shit about yourself then all you have done is created habits of patterns of negative thinking about yourself, which if you think about it sucks donkey ass. Do these ring any bells with you? Do you have 'Oh I never do any good at job interviews' or 'oh I'm always rubbish at quizzes' or 'I never win anything' or the alternative bigging someone else up 'you're better with <insert desired sexual preference> than me' or 'such and such has all the luck'? Do these fly round your brain and spew out your mouth like you are quoting a verse from the bible? Well I say screw that shit, tomorrow think 'I'm super fucking awesome at job interviews' or 'I am the fucking dogs' bollocks at quizzes' or 'I am a golden god with a super <hard/ soft> <insert genital> with the <insert desired sex>', notice how careful I was there lol. By the way I love the phrase 'the dogs bollocks', it just makes no sense, but it sounds like it could be great to have a pair for some reason.

Enjoy yourself, read those two fucking words again slowly. ENJOY YOUR FUCKING SELF. As in 'enjoy' – appreciate, love, adore and 'yourself' as in the self that is you. Stop wishing to be some other tosser as they're probably jealous of something someone else has, maybe even you. You cannot change in to someone else so make the most of who you are. You like plane spotting? Good for you! Go and fill your boots. You don't like sunny days? Fine sit in, and if someone moans about it tell them to fuck off outside and stop disturbing you. *Note my wife hates it when I sit in on a sunny day and I definitely DO NOT have the nerve to tell her to fuck off, they are not dog's, but I do value them. Also, while I'm on, there are millions of dickheads on this planet that can slag you off, don't be an extra one by slagging yourself or other people off as you'll just be doing what other people have done to you in the past and that simply isn't what we're like is it? I'm seeing us as besties now and I don't want to hang around with a spiteful cock womble!

LIVING Chapter 28

Just Say No

Gone Too Far – The Motive

'Saying no to something is actually more powerful
than saying yes' Tom Hanks

I know I've just given you a chapter about saying yes
but there is a time to say the word no, these two little
words can be the key to your future happiness. I have
a toddler at the moment, and he doesn't give a fuck
about pleasing anyone other than himself and why is
this? Because he's a toddler (or the son of Satan joke!)
and he hasn't developed language or thought enough
to give a flying shit about anything other than being
fed, changed, sleep, attracting his mom's attention,
playing with a ball, being made to jump by his brother
or the occasional tickle fest from me. Good for him! At
the moment, we let him get away with this behaviour
because he hasn't had time to learn the rules of life.
However, there is part of me that wants him to keep

some of this independence and desire to please himself. I am a self-confessed people pleaser, at some point my desire to be a 'good boy' has become a full-blown thing for me as an adult which I try to resist with differing levels of success. I know people worse than me and I often feel bad for them, see I'm pleasing the people pleasers now! And I am aware that if I didn't give a fucking shit about anyone like my toddler I'd have no friends and would probably be a psychopath.

I recently found out that people that say 'no' to things that they don't want to do are generally happier and more satisfied than people who do things that they don't wish to do. It kind of makes sense but this means, if you're like me, you have to put up with a short-term awkwardness or worry at the point of saying 'no'. My advice (to me as well as you) and it ties in with the excuses chapter, if you do not want to do something, don't do it. Say no, don't say I might or maybe, say no. You will feel better for not doing it and your friend will appreciate it in the long run too. Be polite but firm and follow through by not doing it. Don't get convinced or cajoled into doing it because that will encourage more of the same behaviours. Be strong and say FUCKING NO (especially to drugs, drunk driving, rape, racism, sexism, bullying and being a general cunt).

LIVING Chapter 29

Remember to Exist

Tracy Chapman – Fast Car

'Enjoy life, it has an expiration date' Zayn Malik

We as a society always seem so bloody busy, working, visiting people, looking after people, hustling and side hustling trying to make extra money while still trying to live a life of meaning and enjoyment for ourselves. We constantly bitch and moan about not having the time to do stuff but guess what? We, I mean me and you have all of the time in the world, if we choose to use it. People my age; 39 now 41 (whoa I've procrastinated since starting this book!) at the time of writing I've heard described as the sandwich generation, as we are the first generation where we have kids later in life, and our parents, thanks to medical science are still alive and may need a certain level of care, meaning that we are not only looking after our children and going to work, running our household, on top of this we are potentially looking after our parents and/ or grandparents as well. All of this activity means that we are forgetting to appreciate and enjoy our own lives. Now again a massive caveat here is that I'm not advocating leaving the old folks to rot or let our kids fend for themselves while we have a foot massage by a big Norwegian guy called Hans, but you do have to remember that your time on the planet shouldn't just be about you supporting others, there has to be something in your life for YOU which is outside of the sphere of care that you provide.

If you are in the predicament I have just described it is time to give yourself permission to have some time to your bloody self. Right now, apart from reading my awesome books, what do you want to do with your free time? Haven't had free time for a while? Then what did you used to do? Where's your happy place? Make time to do it right now. But isn't that selfish I hear you whimper. Firstly, strap a pair on pal, you have the right to be happy as much as the next person, secondly, it's actually not selfish you will be doing everyone around you a massive favour too a) because you'll be happier in yourself meaning you'll moan/ shout less b) because your mind will be in a better place you'll treat the loved ones that you support better because you've had a break. Stop thinking that you have to be some kind of super hero to everyone. If you got hit by a bus, the world would continue, and people would get over it and find someone else to help them or (shockingly) find a way to help themselves. Again, I'm not saying don't care for people I'm just saying you must make time for yourself before you wake up and you're the one being cared for having done absolutely jack shit with your own life!

At my place of work, part of our culture redesign involved adopting Franklyn & Covey's 7 Habits of highly effective people and habit 7 (my favourite habit) is all about 'sharpening the saw'. This one states that if you never stop to sharpen your (figurative) saw it will go blunt or worse break completely, and even if it doesn't break you will become tired from using it as not caring for it makes it harder to use and require more effort by you. This is sad as the tool is meant to be there to help. Another analogy of this, comes from the 90's film Highlander movie franchise (which I loved as a kid) where Sean Connery says to Christopher Lambert 'ashes to ashes, dust to dust, if you don't take it out and use it, it's going to rust', I think he was referring to his penis, but it still works.

But how do I do this when there's so much to do? Well I've already advocated the powers of saying 'no' and 'yes' in the right places and not making excuses, these are a start. But also start to look where you can save time; perhaps batch cooking could help or making one round trip instead of lots of little ones. Also, add your 'you time' to your calendar, set reminders for it, make it happen. You are more likely to do it if you remind yourself and less likely to book something over it if it's booked in. Most importantly stop saying to yourself and others that you don't have the time, this negativity will just lead to your time to being filled and become a self-fulfilling prophecy.

Hopefully, you see why I'm encouraging you to do this, you have a short period of time where you are the fittest you will ever be. The opportunity to maximise your life is right now, this minute you are the youngest you will ever be, oh there it's gone you're now a minute older, that moment is not coming back, neither is this nor this. Think about it you cannot go back in time despite them doing it in a load of movies. Your time is precious and if you don't value it, it will slip away from you.

LIVING Chapter 30

Be Grateful for Everything

Big Yellow Taxi – Joni Mitchell

'There are only two ways to live your life. One is though nothing is a miracle. The other is though everything is a miracle' Albert Einstein

In my first book I referred to the power of gratitude and how by being grateful it brings more positivity in to your world. In this chapter I want to take it a step further and say that you should be grateful for everything not just the positive things in your life but the shitty things too. In the words of Kanye West 'that that don't kill me can only make me stronger' well that's true. Each time you fail, each time you get shit on, you learn another lesson that improves your approach to life. If you live in cotton wool and avoid anything challenging or hard then you will not grow and just remain the same which can't be good (I guess if you're reading this, you probably don't fall into that category?). I grew up in a small town called Tipton and the furthest I would go was West Bromwich another similar minded Black Country town to see my grandparents. When I went to Dudley College (another Black Country town) I grew up a little more and saw more opinions, I then went to Aston University, a city wow! I learnt more and realised that the Black Country wasn't necessarily the same as everywhere else like I'd assumed.

I was scared each time I took a jump to a new place and met new people but each time I did I learnt new things and ways to look at the world. I never really fancied traveling like some of my friends did but I'm sure I would have got a lot out of it. Anyway, I digress during this growing up phase, things went wrong, I had my heart broken by girlfriends and friends alike but looking back, each time I had something shitty happen it allowed me to grow a little bit more. I wasn't grateful for it at the time, but I am grateful for it now, as all of those decisions and lessons led me to having a wife and two beautiful kiddywinks. All the life that unfolds in front of you is there to help you become an ultimate version of you. There are no right or wrong paths just different ones, if you're expecting life to be easy you've picked the wrong game to play and the quicker you accept the shit as well as the good the quicker you'll start to win. Don't go for easy, go for what you want, relish the highs and be gracious in the lows. I think I may have nicked that last sentence from Michael Neill so apologies to him if I did.

Additionally, a few months ago, I fell down the stairs from top to bottom, arse over tit straight down. I shit my pants, no not literally. My life so far and what was left of it flashed before my eyes. Amazingly, I walked away unscathed with just an achy shoulder. I was so grateful that I didn't do any permanent damage or worse still broke my neck or died. It made me realise how things that we take for granted every day could be snatched away from us in instant. I wasn't drunk, I wasn't on drugs, I was paying attention, I just slipped and right there and then I could have lost my ability to move or worse my entire life. That day, I appreciated being able to walk that little bit more and I also realised how lucky I was to be alive and see my wife and two children.

Do you appreciate how lucky you are to be alive? Even if your circumstances aren't that great, you still have the gift of life and that is worth appreciating. I mentioned in my previous book, the work undertaken by my friend Mo Abdel-Gadir undertakes with his Gratitude Pen and Gratitude Lifestyle project. The premise is that the more grateful we are the more positive things there are in our life for us to be grateful about coming into our lives as a result. When you're going about your day to day life try to appreciate what you have, it may not be exactly what you want, but it's what you've got right now and there's lots of people who would love what you have. I heard a really good phrase that pertains to this 'it's not getting what you want, it's wanting what you've got'. This also goes for appreciating people for their differences to you, instead of trying to change someone so that they're more like you, notice how they're different to you and how differing views in the world help you have a more rounded view and could even expand your horizons beyond your own front door.

LIVING Chapter 31

Check Yo Self Before You Wreck Yo Self

Check yo self (before yo wreck yo self) – Ice Cube

'I am a victim of my own behaviour' Henry R Brandt

Wow what a dad (and frankly shit) title for a chapter, great song though, fuck it lets carry on we haven't got time in our lives to analyse it. And that my friend is the whole point I'm trying to make in this book. We don't have time to worry about how shit the title of the chapter is, we don't have time to argue and fight with random strangers on the internet, we don't have time for this sentence, but it was required for you to get my point. Also, for the astute and/ or cocky amongst you I know that this contradicts the last chapter about us having time but I'm sure you can see the nuance I am going for. We have time for the things we want to do but we don't have time to waste. The music is on so get dancing before the lights come on or go off whichever.

Goals and desires are great but if you don't do anything towards them then they aren't worth the paper that they are written on (if you've written them down). I always wanted to be an author (I still do) and sometimes I find it hard to sit down to my laptop and write even one word. Today for instance, I just cannot be fucking arsed to write this, however my desire to be an author and my goal to finish my second book is keeping me here. How are you managing to keep writing, I hear you ask? Well if I thought I had to write the whole book to publishing standard today, as in 50,000 words which is my aim to double the word count of the last book then I would not be able to do it. My head would go fuck that, go and play frisbee in the garden, hell do the washing up, do anything rather than writing a full book.

The way I motivate myself to keep going is to break the activities into bitesize chunks. I was on roughly 28,000 words when I started today, and I decided to challenge myself to get to 30,000 words by the end of the day. A smaller number than the whole piece but a good chunk towards my target that I can be proud of for one day. Sometimes when I do this I fall short and get to about 500 words, most times I get going and struggle to stop and end up exceeding my goal by thousands. The hardest part for me is the starting part, which is why I do things to keep me coming back. I make sure my seat is as comfortable as possible, I poor myself a nice drink (could range from a glass of squash to something more alcoholic) and put a few cushions behind me. I then get my laptop and switch it on in this comfy environment. This then means for the next half an hour even if crap words come out on the screen, I have got a nice place to sit and a drink to hand. The last part of my routine is to offer myself a reward for doing this work (which I have no guarantee of ever being paid for), the reward isn't massive, but it might be, if you do 2000 words you don't have to do any exercise today or you can have a BBQ later. It's rarely got any monetary value as I save that for the end of the book where I promise myself a gift such as a new watch or gadget. These rewards, though small are far outweighed at the end when there is a finished book but kept me going on the long journey. Bit like a service station KFC or a beer when you've finished a long drive.

These rewards are in place to make me achieve my goal in small intervals. The desire to be a published author, the goal to finish my second book, the short-term goal of 2000 words and then short-term reward of a takeaway or treat which makes me get started in the first place. Just to be clear, I have a good job and do not need the money from book sales, I have no publishing deal so there is no contractual pressure. I have already published one book, so it is not about that. This is my own motivation to kick myself up the ass and achieve something. Do you ever kick your own ass to achieve your goal or desire?

Let's try an experiment. This Saturday morning at 9am get your watch or your phone and set an alarm for every hour starting with 10am for the whole day until 5pm. Next get a pad and a pen to write on. Now, every time the alarm goes off I want you to write down exactly what you've done in that hour and how many minutes you honestly spent doing it. You can miss out toilet and food breaks but everything else write down. If you've spoken to your neighbour write it down, if you've played on your phone write it down, if you've ahem pleased yourself write a code for that just in case someone else reads it. At 5pm I want you to look at your list, and tick how many things you've done towards achieving your goals even if it's in a small way. Then I want you to tick the things where you've wasted time, by wasted I don't mean time with your family or driving somewhere

I mean done basically bugger all e.g. watching a film you've already seen or playing a game on your phone. Next, I want you to total the time you took to achieve your goal and the amount you took doing fuck all. I then want you to multiply those two figures by 7, 28 and 365 to show you the amount of time that you will spend trying to achieve your goals for a week, month and year respectively and then how much time you have available where you could be striving towards your goal or desire. I'm guessing because you're reading this and doing the experiment that you may game the system and do a little bit towards the goal and feel ok about yourself, but if you are truly honest and if I'm truly honest with myself I spend very little time trying to achieve my goals. Why is this? Is it fear of failure? Is it laziness? Is it apathy that you or I will get around to doing it one day. Well again I am here to tell you that as a 41 year old man, I have wasted a lot of time procrastinating and though I am not old I do feel that time is slipping away from me and there are somethings I can't do now that I could when I was younger, some through lack of desire but some through just being older and a bit creakier. Don't let time slip through your fingers.

LIVING Chapter 32

Keep Smiling and Laughing

Smile Like You Mean It – The Killers

'Laughter is the best medicine, unless you're diabetic then insulin comes pretty high on the list' Jasper Carrot

Whenever I see my mom and dad they are always smiling and laughing or trying to make me laugh. I thought everyone was like this when I was younger as they were my only reference point but as I grew up I began to realise that they are quite unusual in this perpetual happiness. The other difference in them is that they always seem quite well (even when they're ill). I'm not underestimating that this might be a) rose tinted glasses on my part or b) a small act on theirs however, friends and family have commented on how happy they always seem, so I think it might be more than an act for my benefit. Besides I'm 41 so I'm passed the age that they need to protect me from the truth. Regardless this state of wellbeing that they emit, I think must have some part to do with their happiness. My dad is one of a handful of men in his whole county where they live that has been given 12 months to come back for a check-up by his doctor which for his age (69) is pretty impressive, despite him drinking alcohol quite often and having a high salt intake. The other thing I've noticed is that this laughter and happiness is infectious. When I see them, I feel happier and I always remember dad cracking jokes at weddings and even on hospital visits to see ill members of our family, and everyone (even the patient) would seem to perk up.

Observing this, I feel I have picked up some of this behaviour, I rarely moan about things and always try to make my friends laugh when I see them regardless of their frame of mind. Life is too short to take yourself seriously all of the time, I get that not everyone is jolly and laughing and I am not advocating fake laughter and forced fun, but I guess I am advocating lightening up on things. Taking time to smell the roses and savouring the small stuff rather than being uptight. *Takes drag of massive spliff 'chilllllllllllllllllllllllllll man!'*. I don't do drugs by the way. Anyway, the reason I started to write this chapter was because my friend Mark from work has just sent me a hilarious video of a man trying his home made limoncello. Lol. He spits it out as it's so bitter and it really made me belly chuckle, I'm chuckling now thinking about it, guess you needed to be there. But anyway, the feeling of this uncontrollable laughter made me feel great. It reminds me of the old adage 'laughter is the best medicine'. Actually, I've just Googled that phrase, and this is what came up...

Laughter decreases stress hormones and increases immune cells and infection-fighting antibodies, thus improving your resistance to disease. Laughter triggers the release of endorphins, the body's natural feel-good chemicals. Endorphins promote an overall sense of well-being and can even temporarily relieve pain.

So, if you're feeling a bit blue watch a comedy, it might make you feel better. Conversely, and alarmingly, sadness and depression can lead to physical illness such as headaches and body aches and pain. Reasons to be cheerful 1, 2, 3.

LIVING Chapter 33

The Shit That Numbs the Pain Also Causes It

This is a Low – Blur

'Through self-discipline comes freedom' Aristotle

I know I know another unbelievably long title for a chapter, but I'm trying to hammer these messages home. Gambling, drink, drugs and sex are all of the things that are (hopefully) unavailable to children in today's society. So, is it any surprise that when humans get to the age of being able to get these things that shit starts to get complicated? No course not duh! It's because these things are bad for you that you aren't allowed them. But like the apple in the garden of Eden because you can't have it you want it even more, so when you finally get told that you can have it you go mental; forbidden apple everywhere! However, once you've had too much of this apple you feel like crap (remember it's bad for you!) and you think 'ooh that shit hurt I'll numb the pain of that with I know, more of that shit' which then causes more shit, and you think you know what I need more of to make me feel better more of that fucking shit and this cycle continues. Fuck people come on, it's not rocket science. I have used two of these (gambling and alcohol) I was a gambling addict and as shit as it made me feel I continued doing it and the more I chased my money, the more I drank to numb the pain of losing all my money. You could say it was a vicious circle.

If you take drugs to get over pain from your childhood or relationships or some other shit, the more drugs you take the shitter you'll feel so the more you'll take. Insert junk food, caffeine, sex, destructive relationships and all of them have this cyclical nature about them. You cane them, you get fucked up, you cane them to get over getting fucked up, rinse and repeat. Right I'm here to say FUCKING STOP! If you got fucked up last night (in any of the above way) today is a new day so give it a rest for today, tomorrow you'll wake up without a hangover/ regret or whatever, the day after that you'll feel even better, you might notice that your house needs a tidy or you've enjoyed a good night sleep, or you don't wheeze as you breathe as much. Stop blaming your shit on old stuff, you're the one keeping it going!

LIVING Chapter 34

Don't Be Marty McFly

Yesterday – The Beatles

'Forget the past' Nelson Mandela

Back to the Future was me and my friends' favourite film as a kid, the thought that you could go backwards and forwards in time to make things better or change mistakes was so tantalising and probably attributes to its success. Well I'm sorry to say that it is just a film, with a script, sets and actors it's not real. Ok thanks for that what's your point? Well a common theme throughout this book is to live in the moment and is a driving principle of mindfulness. When we're regretting the past or worrying about the future we're time travelling in our minds which if you think about it is totally pointless. The past is gone, and we cannot change anything in it, it is never coming back, what we did or didn't do is unchangeable, so fuck regret and grudges, return to the present.

Same with worrying about the future, the future doesn't exist yet. You may never get to the event you're imagining being good or bad. I'm sick of people saying 'I can't wait for summer' or 'I'll be happier when I've got X or Y' but by wishing for these things they're robbing themselves of happiness right now. This is different to making plans and striving for your goals, because you're assuming that this future activity will be better or worse than what you've got. There is also a potential for the future event not to live up to your imagination or simply be not as good as expected. You've then spent your precious time fantasising of what's to come while missing out on what could have been good here and now. There are so many opportunities in this moment that we miss out upon because of our regrets and future looking. Seize the day savour the moment, give yourself permission to enjoy the here and now.

LIVING Chapter 35

Suck It Up!

Jealous Guy – Roxy Music

'Jealousy is the stupid child of pride or the illness of a madman' Pierre Beaumarchais

I toyed with 'Don't be a cunt' for the title of this chapter but I think the one that I used was slightly more poetic, don't you think? But I'm sure that you can get the general gist of what it means. Putting it simply while living your life and doing what you want to do, don't be a wanker to other people and don't shit on other people's dreams. Bizarrely, I have just been crying with laughter to outtakes of the Ricky Gervais Netflix comedy; After Life, a comedy drama about a suicidal guy living his life after his wife died of cancer. It's a brilliant watch and it puts a lot of the menial things you worry about and even some of the bigger things into perspective. In the first series he takes his misery out on everyone else and becomes very spiteful towards other seemingly happy people. Putting other people down because things in his life weren't as good because he'd suffered the loss. The best part about the show, in my opinion, is the fact that it shows flashbacks of his life when he was happy with his wife through the form of old videos they had recorded together. This juxtaposition of the miserable with the happy, serves to remind us of the different experiences of life. Also, his brother-in-law, who he works for is also experiencing his marriage breaking down as well as his sister dying but he chooses to be nice and supportive to others. It is beautifully written and devilishly funny and if you get the chance you should watch it to see how differently grief can be handled and also how destroying someone else doesn't make you any happier. It also makes you realise that you don't know what is going on in people's personal life, so be kind or at least not a twat to others.

I believe that one of the biggest causes of animosity to others is because of jealousy. Jealousy is an odd thing and I find that I have to occasionally manage mine. I guess it fits with the selfish gene analogy by Richard Dawkins; that I want my life and my families' life to be successful, so my genes can continue on the planet long after I've departed. If someone is successful sometimes I think 'oh why wasn't that me' which I then replace with 'good for them, it wasn't me because that isn't what I've been working hard on like them'. When I was younger I was always pleased for other people and then as I got older and things I perceived to be negative started happening to me, sometimes on a regular basis, I would end up being secretly resentful of someone else's good fortune. But this jealousy was mostly misplaced, don't get me wrong sometimes things are not fair, if you have ever been to or performed in a battle of the bands you'll know the hidden politics behind them of whether a band has more people there or friends with an organiser leading to possibly one of the not so good bands winning. But on the whole jealousy is a pointless and painful exercise. Pointless because if it was meant to be you it would have been you (even in my battle of the bands misery, it wasn't meant to be me). Painful because the only person feeling bad is yourself.

A lot of the time, unfortunately it can be uncontrollable, but you can manage (and choose) how you react to it. If you choose to try to sabotage someone else then you are a massive bellend (see Simpsons episode: When Flanders Failed), if you choose to share your annoyance then it makes you look bitter and resentful and if you hold it in eventually it will pop out somewhere else, which may not be your best moment especially if it is in front of the person the feelings relates to. So, what do I do about it then Einstein? Well I just so happen to have a five point 'suck it up' plan.

1) Acknowledge the success in your mind, Mr or Mrs X has done well at X.

2) Process what this success means to you, I would have liked that for myself or I am disappointed that it wasn't me.

3) Process what the success means to the person achieving it, they have obviously worked hard for it or even if not, they may deserve it for some other reason. Have you put the effort in? Have you made the sacrifices that Mr or Mrs X has?

4) Process what the success means in the grand scheme of things towards your and the successful person's life. Is it life changing, and could you achieve the same? Is it what you want out of life? Or are you just jealous that they have succeeded where you have not?

5) If you could achieve it be inspired to replicate it, if you couldn't achieve it, take a deep breath and re-focus on the things you're good at and what you want to achieve out of life. We are all unique and what is meant for us will come to us. What is not will not. Suck it up!

As I've just turned 41 I sometimes feel jealous of my younger friends. Not that I want them not to be young, but I do wish I was their age and had my life in front of me again like they have. But then I remind myself that I had a great time at their age and even the youngest friend I have will eventually be my age now and I'll be a lot older and/ or dead when that happens.

I'm not for one moment condoning jealous behaviour, but I do see why, unchecked it would come out as anger or spitefulness. Jim Parsons (Sheldon from Big Bang Theory) is quoted to have said 'someone else's success is not your failure' and that is so fucking true, me writing this book does not mean that someone else can't write a book and the success of that book does not impact or take away from my book's achievement. For instance, things aren't binary, where the consequence of one book being purchased means that another book is unable to be purchased. So, there is no need to resent other people doing the same or similar to you if they have success.

I want you to remember that the people around you are people too. They have hopes and dreams and unless you're living in a post-Covid zombie apocalypse where we now have to forage and kill for food, someone else's success does not detract from your potential for success and should not make you feel inferior. Despite what glossy magazines and Instagram feeds would have you believe there are no perfect people in the world. Everyone has their own problems and hang ups, and this has been shown recently with some high-profile suicides in the press which I won't go into. My wake-up call to this knowledge came when I was younger and just starting out playing in bands. Feeder were massive and had beaten the other pop drivel to number one in the charts (for the younger readers this is something that used to mean something!), shortly after this success their drummer, that lived in New York with his model wife killed himself. This man had everything I wanted in life and he took his own life. Why? It instantly changed my perspective on what success was. When I was younger, I always wondered why people kill themselves, I have since got the gist when I felt real pain but there was always a bit of me (and still is) that thinks, why not just pick up sticks and go travelling or move to a new house or emigrate? I guess some things are more than just your physical location, as when you get to the new destination, you are still there in your head. Doh! When I have felt suicidal in the past despite seemingly having everything to the outside world I could totally see why he did what he did, the things you have don't block out the negative thoughts fucking you up.

Just in case here is the Samaritans number: 116-123

Look, I am sure you're perfectly lovely people and jealousy is something that never happens to you (snigger) but if you find yourself listening to someone with an idea and you start to dissuade them from doing it because it's 'too risky' or 'would never work', I want you to stop right there and think to yourself is this advice pissing on someone's chips or if you're feeling brave, 'am I being a dream shattering cunt here?' Remember, they are not you and you are not a fortune teller, you should only give supportive advice rather than putting them off doing it because you'll potentially look bad compared to them if they succeed with whatever it is they're talking about. Their success is not going to detract from you as you have your own skills and flaws and so will they whether they're successful or not. I have friends on both ends of the spectrum, ones that are really supportive of everything I do and ones where they take the piss out of everything I do. I must remember that their views are their views and probably land somewhere in between the two but if you find yourself giving 'advice' that stops someone from doing it then don't. You have no clue whether it will work or not. Instead, why not support your friend, give them encouragement, offer to invest in their idea, nick a bit of reflected glory. You might become rich, or more likely develop stronger relationships with your nearest and dearest. Alternatively, you could use this jealousy, to ask yourself what it is that you would like to do so you feel less bitter about others' potential success.

LIVING Chapter 36

Abuse

Acrobat – Maximo Park

'Abuse is not love, abuse is about control' Domestic Violence Survivor

I had a big discussion with my Editor; Ameesha about including this chapter, as I had placed a throwaway few lines about not staying with an abusive partner in one of the first drafts of this book and even though I'd written the words, every time I read them, they felt callous and jarring. Ameesha agreed and we planned this chapter to be not about victim shaming or virtue signalling but to help people in abusive relationships realise that if they accept this negative behaviour towards them, their partner, relative or friend can waste, ruin or even take their life and if this applies to you, then you deserve better and you should leave before it's too late.

I have been in two mentally abusive relationships, I loved the two individuals and looking back do not understand how they became abusive. They both started out loving and caring partners, and that's probably why I tolerated the abuse for so long. I look back at the things that were said to me and there is no way I would accept that from anyone today, but as I believed I was 'in love' with them I accepted the control, albeit minor to begin with and accepted them back each time they would leave me because I hadn't done what they'd asked (not seen my friends, or replied to a text from the opposite sex) and then each time they returned I would submit another piece of myself to them. If I had parties or gatherings, invariably they would either cause a drama beforehand, so we didn't go, or argue with me while our friends and family waited patiently for us to finish or excuse ourselves. All of this leading to me not wanting to go out with anyone else through fear of embarrassment.

They would question me over and over again about my interactions with others, obsessively asking me details to the point where I would invite them in to the conversation to save living my life twice and risking further hassle. Sarcastic comments about my clothes or my hobbies, led me to becoming withdrawn and impacted my mental wellbeing with me needing a counsellor for some time after, but I had got other shit going on so I'm not blaming them entirely for this. It's also worth noting that while I was in these relationships I felt my behaviour change towards them, one was upset so much that I laughed when she cried as it happened so often, from an outsider looking in that must seem awful, but my reaction was masking pain and trying to gain a little control back of what I had lost. If my life was a movie then it was Falling Down the realisation at the end where he asks, 'I'm the bad guy?'.

Luckily, my friends stuck around and helped me, but they could have easily got bored of seeing me arguing or cancelling last minute on them. The reason why I've shared this is to stop you from wasting any more of your time while waiting for someone you love to return to their loving self that they displayed at the start like I was and wasted six years of my life. You do not owe anyone ANYTHING. You do not have to believe the negative things that people say about you as a lot of what is said is out of fear of losing you, so they undermine your self-worth to keep you with them. My rule of thumb is if you wouldn't want to see them once you've died and gone to heaven then they're not worth staying with now here on earth while you have the only guaranteed existence.

I've hidden these contact details here just in case you need it then I promise I'll get back on with the book.

Freephone National Domestic Abuse Helpline, run by Refuge
0808 200 0247
www.nationaldahelpline.org.uk

LIVING Chapter 37

Be Water, Not Stone

Waterfall – Stone Roses

'Flexibility is the key to stability' John Wooden

Close your eyes, by the way I do realise I need to edit this for if it ever gets published on audio book otherwise I'm going to be responsible for a lot of road deaths if people do as I ask while they are driving! Then the title of the book will be really accurate. Back to closing your eyes, I want you to picture who you are. Simple right? But just contemplate it and then write down what you thought, again not if you're driving or operating heavy machinery. I'm guessing you may have a few fundamentals that you think of that are the same as everyone else like you were born, you are a human, you have a name, you breathe oxygen and drink water, you have a gender whether it be the one on your birth certificate or the one you identify as. But the rest of the things that make up you will be solely unique to you. This to me is the definition of you. If I were to do it I would say:

Adam, human, pale skin (cause I'm looking at my hands lit up by a laptop at 6 in the fackin' morning!), dad, husband, fairly bright, joker, centre of attention, rough round the edges, good heart, and then I'd go on to some of the things I do; craft beer drinker, part time writer, full time ass hole, KFC munching, good bloke.

I genuinely did the above, without thinking too much (I did it without thinking wahoo!). Anyway, if I look at that list apart from 'husband' and 'writer' on there I have been everything else since I was 32, that's since 2012 when my first son was born. But, if I look even harder at the list, and remove dad, husband and craft beer drinker, I've pretty much been the same guy since about 16; back then I drank cheap cider. Thinking about it (there I go again), this is probably why people get imposter syndrome, if your essence is the same since you were 16 or younger, why would you feel that you've grown up and especially grown up enough to do an 'adult job'?

Why am I talking about this? Well, have you ever known anyone that has completely changed their appearance or way of being in the world? You know like a fat person just woke up one day and started (and succeeded) to get thin. Or someone who hasn't had a job for years all of a sudden decides to go to night school and gets a decent job and makes a success of themselves? Or the uptight business man that retires to go hiking. My epiphany came when my first was born, in 2010, two years before he arrived, I was a 30-year-old man child. I was defined by drinking, gambling and playing video games and if I think back I don't think I valued my life because I'd never really stopped to think about it because for some random reason I thought I was going to die before I turned 30. Not due to suicide or depression or those thoughts came and passed like I'm sure they do for others, I just thought because I do all this random messing about, sleeping outside, getting kicked out of pubs etc that my life was going one way and it wasn't up. I had a job, I had the trappings of a nice life, house, car, cat and girlfriend but nothing to tie me down, and I thought that I liked it.

Fast forward two years and two relationships later, my first son arrived with a thud, his mom told me she was pregnant (we hadn't known each other for very long and she lived in London) and boom! I drove back to the West Midlands like when the guy in Lock Stock and Two Smoking Barrels loses all of his friend's money at poker. Me, a dad what the actual fuck, his mom living miles away what the actual fuck. I walked into my house, I was living with my folks at the time and they were sitting there watching something like Who Wants to be a Millionaire without a care in the world. They sat up 'you look pale', I said 'she's pregnant', 'what are you going to do' said my mom. 'We're going to have a baby' I said back. We were all shocked? Why? I was thirty fucking two! Because I was a drunken twat with an unborn child that lived in London, and I definitely wasn't mature enough to be a dad. I knew it and they knew it, that night we polished off a full bottle of whisky as a family.

Cue the arrival of my little chap, and as I held this little stranger in my arms, and though I didn't instantly recognise him like I thought I would, as I'd seen on the movies, everything changed. I gave up online gambling and eventually casino gambling, I gave up drinking all of my weekends away, I sorted my finances out, paid off my credit card and started working harder at work and importantly I never slept in a bus stop or under a bush again. It was like someone had switched a switch and I had a purpose; to love and protect this squidgy ball of smiling skin, and this meant I had to survive to do so, which meant giving up the Darwin Award lifestyle I'd been living up until then. It wasn't conscious, it just happened. I had my epiphany and he was small and squidgy. Now don't get me wrong, now and again I occasionally gamble or drink too much or whatever but the fundamental changes of being responsible have lasted for the last 9 years and I'm sure they will last for a good while longer now my new little chap has arrived.

I'm sharing this story for two purposes, 1) it highlights that we can get stuck in a rut, a good one or a bad one but 2) it shows that we, me or you can change right now IF we want or need to. Don't get me wrong, it's hard to break old habits (my dad always says to me leopards don't change their spots) but like the Groundhog Day chapter, you can change by making a habit of making the change you want or even make a habit of changing so you never remain the same at all. When I woke up this morning and had this chapter on my mind (thanks weird dreams!) I had the great analogy of the fact that adults are made of 55-60% water and our cells are renewing all of the time and I contemplated that perhaps, we start to die when we start to solidify and don't try new experiences. Interestingly, while researching this chapter I have learnt that babies are 75% water and it got me thinking that maybe that's because they're fluid and developing their personality, whereas as we grow up we become more set in who we are and solidify making it harder for us to change.

If every day is the same what is the point in living another day the same, except on lockdown where this has been a survival mechanism, even then it doesn't need to be completely the same day just a similar location. I saw a brilliant meme on Instagram today that said, 'Don't live the same year 75 times and call it a life', how powerful is that? There is a world of possibilities out there, yet most of us while away in the same job, with the same friends, visiting the same families and going on the same holidays to the same locations year in and year out. Why?! Comfort? Predictability? Or did we solidify at a certain point?

What I want you to take from this chapter, is like the old phrase 'if you do what you've always done, you'll get what you've always got' and if you're getting what you don't want, which you probably are if you've picked up a book called 'YOU ARE GOING TO FUCKING DIE'. You have the ability to change the outcome of your life today. You can attempt to change your circumstances by changing your thoughts. It doesn't have to be an epiphany like I had, it may just be that you decide to hang around with a negative character in your life less, it may be that you change your job from an accountant to an RSPCA officer, it could be anything. You can be who you want to be, and you can change that today, if you're straight let your parents know, they'll be ok with it. If you want to join the circus do that. If you're sick of having no friends be less of a dick! If you've got too many friends be more of a dick! I want you to know it can be done, and if you change and don't like it, go back to how you were before. Be more like water than stone.

DYING Chapter 38

Thoughts from Anthony & Steve

The Middle – Jimmy Eat World

No quote as this chapter is about quotes

You know these guys! Ant and Steve from the pub, not really these are two quotes from the acclaimed actor and Oscar winning Anthony Hopkins and Steve (I changed the world with the iPhone) Jobs. Most authors like to plop famous quotes at the start of their chapters and I'm sure you've noticed that I do too. I used to love it in Frasier when they put a quote at the start of each act and you had to work out what it was going to be about. Well I've decided to dedicate a whole chapter to two of the quotes themselves because I'm just that type of guy. I must caveat that I've got these quotes from the internet, so they may not be totally accurate or even said by them, but I like to think they were as they are awesome and would be gutted if some spotty teenager had duped me. Not only because I respect what they've done I'd also be gutted for the spotty teenager for not getting any credit for writing such beautifully poignant motivating speeches.

Firstly, Anthony Hopkins in case you've been living under a rock is one of the most famous British actors of all time, and probably most famous for his blood swilling role as Hannibal Lector in the Silence of the Lambs. At the time of writing, Anthony Hopkins is still alive (and just won another Best Actor Oscar), and Steve Jobs has sadly passed away.

Sir Anthony Hopkins CBE tweeted:

"None of us are getting out of here alive, so please stop treating yourself like an afterthought.
Eat the delicious food.
Walk in the sunshine.
Jump in the ocean.
Say the truth that you're carrying in your heart like hidden treasure.
Be silly. Be kind. Be weird.
There's no time for anything else."

I mean just wow. He captures what I've been using all these swear words for perfectly. He even uses the term 'afterthought' – after thought remember me banging on about our lives being made up of our thoughts. Love it on many levels. There is no point waiting until tomorrow, live in the moment. Try everything (that's not painful, illegal or disgusting) once! Why not? People may laugh, but who gives a shit? People will be disappointed or talk about you but remember the famous adage from Bette Davis and later resurrected by Gary Oldman;

'what other people think of me, is none of my business' and they're right. People will think good or bad of you regardless of what you do, but not doing something because you think that someone else would think so is (if you think about it) totally fucked up! I know that some people will hate this book, I hope some people will love it. Do either of those things put me off writing it, well kind of, but fuck them I'm being silly, being unkind and being weird. Oh, it says kind, shit I hope we do get a second chance to life as I've been a cheeky little shit for most of this one. All I'm trying to get at is, ask yourself seriously, 'why not'? to any question whatever that question may be.

Steve Jobs wrote:

"Remembering that I'll be dead soon is the most important tool I've ever encountered to help me make the big choices in life.

Almost everything--all external expectations, all pride, all fear of embarrassment or failure--these things just fall away in the face of death, leaving only what is truly important.

Remembering that you are going to die is the best way I know to avoid the trap of thinking you have something to lose. You are already naked. There is no reason not to follow your heart.

No one wants to die. Even people who want to go to heaven don't want to die to get there. And yet, death is the destination we all share. No one has ever escaped it, and that is how it should be, because death is very likely the single best invention of life. It's life's change agent. It clears out the old to make way for the new."

I know that this is quite a depressing quote, especially in these times of uncertainty with Coronavirus knocking about and all. But look at what he was trying to purvey to us. He is highlighting the fleeting nature of our existence. He is holding a torch to what is true, we are only here for a brief period of time and should embrace our passions, our loved ones and our moments with all our might. We should live every minute as if it's our last and be grateful for all of the events that unfold before us rather than shying away. As a species we have forgotten how to live in the pursuit of safety. Steve Jobs sadly died alone but look at what he did with his life, he spearheaded an electronic revolution and left the planet knowing he'd achieved something that would influence mankind forever what an immortality project he had!

DYING Chapter 39

A Brief Look at Death in Other Cultures

Hurt – Jonny Cash

'I'm death, and I make sure everyone is equal'
Jacob Grimm

According to my Dad and backed up by Wikipedia for a change, Tibetan Buddhists undertake something called a 'Sky Burial', intrigued? Well put that sandwich down before I tell you. This is the practice of cutting up dead humans that died naturally and then leaving them at the top of mountains for eagles and vultures to eat (some even throw the 'meat' up!).

Anyway, this takes place in other countries (don't worry you won't spot this happening on your sponsored three peaks challenge in Snowdown!) it is performed by Indian Parsi people. It may seem gross but if you think about it, it's quite a good way to recycle our used-up vessel, which is exactly what Buddhists think it is because they're all about the soul and essence rather than the body. According to Wiki again, the Tibetan monks see this as a representation of the impermanence of life. Basically, after you go you become bird food so don't worry about shit, I think is where they're going but related to back to your (or my) worries, if you thought you were gonna be a KFH for some vulture on some convoluted sky drive-thru you'd probably worry less about whether someone at work doesn't like you or if your cousin has got a better house than you. You'd probably think fuck it, I'll get on with having a laugh with my loved ones. Personally, I would love to be buried like this, maybe I could ask my wife to leave me on the bird box and let the two horny pigeons that occupy the crematorium trees behind my house to have me as an 'all you can eat buffet'. Sure, that little shit squirrel with a probably have a nibble on my toes too (it was too obvious to say my nuts lol).

Moving swiftly on, I'm sure you've all seen the Day of the Dead festival or *Día de Muertos* in Mexico from films such as Coco or one of the Daniel Craig James Bond films that I can't be arsed to Google. This is a national celebration where people dress up as brightly coloured skeletons, tell stories and display pictures of their loved ones that have passed away. The premise being that for this one day of the year if the photograph is still displayed or their name is still mentioned then they can still return to their loved ones, it is only when they are forgotten to be remembered (yes I meant that) that they have passed fully into the afterlife. This event reminds people of two things, the fact that people die and of the dead themselves. Both of these things can't help but impact the behaviours of the participants as you could argue that by wanting to be remembered by the living once you have gone, you must endeavour to make a positive impact on people while you're alive. The thought of passed loved ones helps sharpen the mind as to the briefness of life allowing the individual for the lead up and day itself to contemplate one's own life and to weigh up if they are achieving what they want to achieve with the breath that they have been given.

I know it was quite a brief chapter, but I just wanted you to realise that not all cultures have the standard church yard or crematorium funeral with a wake. This couple of examples highlight how death is a part of life and that by acknowledging it (even celebrating it) can take away some of the seriousness that we've placed on our being here. By talking about death and seeing the dead in this way can set us free and remind ourselves of the time that they were alive rather than the moment that they died. Interestingly there is a relatively new trend for people to leave flowers at road traffic accident scenes. I wonder if this is to do with religion becoming less prevalent, as well as wanting to tribute to the person where they were last alive. I know that this has been talked about in local authorities, as the creation of shrines on busy roads can be dangerous in itself, but on the other hand it does serve to remind other drivers of the perils of the road. In France they place metal black figures in the side of the road called 'morts' to highlight the number killed on the road. My mom thought they looked like ghosts so probably doing their job well then.

DYING Chapter 40

Write a Fucking Will

Going for Gold – Shed Seven

'The wife's mother said, 'when you're dead I'll dance on your grave'. I said, 'good I'm being buried at sea' Les Dawson passed on by Ray Jones (my dad)

Ok this is one of the most practical and important chapters within this book. The title says it all, no matter how much or how little you've got make a fucking will. Why Adam, you've told me shit doesn't matter when I'm dead, well this fucking does ok! I have been to too many funerals where the lack of a will has left feelings frayed and in certain circumstances put the finances of those left behind in jeopardy (why is there an 'o' in jeopardy?). Wills are there for that reason, so that your will is seen out when you are not there to describe things in person. I'm not talking some crazy ass will like in Brewster's Millions (if you haven't seen it, watch it) I'm talking about a statement of where your assets (your belongings and property) go to as well as any wishes and funds for your disposal i.e. your funeral costs.

Ok so you get the premise of this book? None of us are immortal but once we're dead other people (your wife, husband, kids, significant other etc) live on and for that reason you need to make sure that while you're alive, if you can afford to is ensure that stuff of yours is passed on. If you think about it, just think how chuffed they will be when they receive something of yours whether it be in the form of money, charity donation or item of significance. I can't tell you what to leave to whom, one I don't know you and two I don't know what you have and three I don't know your relationship with your nearest and/ or dearest. What I do know is, there's no point in being selfish when creating it, as guess what, you'll be dead, and my best guess suggests that you won't see what happens to the stuff anyway. If you have two sons and you get on with one better than other split your estate in half and leave something special to both, you shouldn't expect to get on with both the same but I'm sure both have equal merit, after all they both came from you, and it's not their fault that that bit of sperm was the one that had more in common with their mom or some shit like that. Be specific in your will, leave nothing to chance, money makes people do crazy shit especially when coupled with grief/ relief so ensure what you have goes exactly where you want before you surprisingly pop your clogs or lose the ability to decide and some greedy bastard spots an opportunity like I have witnessed people do in my family.

Remember people are selfish and will act in a way that suits themselves especially if you are not there to see it or verify it. Very briefly when I worked at West Midlands Fire Service as part of our road safety campaigns at valentine's day we ran a stall called 'For My Girlfriend' it had hundreds of red roses on it and plonked it in the middle of a local college. The message was that no matter how much someone loves you, if two people are in a car crash together the driver will swerve to save themselves rather than the passenger. Fucked up right? But true, somewhere deep within us is an innate desire to live over and above those around us, and that kicks in when there's no time to make a decision and think of the consequences. Ponder that for a moment, so even if you know that everyone loves each other (they probably do), still make sure that you're clear on who gets what. I haven't made one so I'm a fucking hypocrite, but I will this week and hopefully before I publish this book.

DYING Chapter 41

Get a Bucket List

The Bucket – Kings of Leon

'One day you will wake up and there won't be any more time to do the things you've always wanted. Do it Now' Paulo Coelho

Firstly, do you know what a bucket list is? For those of you that don't know a bucket list is a list of things you'd like to have done by the time you kick the bucket (die). Get it? They can be big things or little things, that you've always wanted to do. Secondly, do you have one? You may not call it that, but do you have a list of stuff that you'd like to achieve or experience before the time that you are no more?

Most people have big things that they want to do on theirs; like parachute or visit the pyramids but some people have more realistic desires like eat in a Michelin Starred restaurant or see the sun rise, but they can be anything really. A couple of mine include going to Machu Picchu and skydiving. I recommend writing one as it can help you work out if you're doing what you want to or doing what someone else wants you to do. Writing down your goals and keeping them with you and reviewing them often gives you more chance of achieving them. Also, telling other people what they are also gives you more of a shot of achieving them. The main reason I advocate getting a bucket list is so that you have something to strive for, as lack of purpose in life has been linked to addiction and depression and if you think about it, if we haven't got anything to do or live for, then what's the point in living?

Despite the title of my last book my mom and dad have impressed me where it comes to this type of stuff. Firstly, they practice what they preach, as they retired and had the balls to move to a different country (France) where they didn't speak the language, secondly more recently they have both signed up to Open University courses that they'd been interested in for years and my dad did the largest zip wire in Wales with me and my wife last year as well. They are active and on the whole happy people and I put a lot of it down to them having drive in their life to do something or achieve something and not stuck in a rut but constantly moving forward even if it is at a slower pace than when they were younger, and I think that's cool. I find it odd that people create their bucket list in the latter years of their life and the majority of the people will be doing this because they have spent their lives working and waiting to do these dreams.

Finally, there's an episode of The Simpsons (I love Simpsons references) where Homer believes he's eaten a poisonous fish and he's told that he only has 24 hours to live and it stayed with me. He realised how fleeting his life was and how important his family was to him all things up until that point he had ignored or taken for granted. Comically, he tried to complete all of his life goals in a short period of time with hilarious consequences. *Spoiler Alert* It turns out he didn't eat poison and doesn't die, and he goes back to normal, but this cartoon holds truth for most of us; we take life and our families for granted and only appreciate them when we think we are going to lose either or both. Make sure your bucket list contains the normal things as well as the extreme cool things. A hug from my wife, two sons, mom and dad are way more up there than skydiving or some other crazy shit I can tell ya. Choose wisely my friends.

DYING Chapter 42

Tie Up Loose Ends

Living Years – Mike and the Mechanics

'Don't wait until it's too late to say I love you'
Stana Katic

When I was younger my grandparents gave me pocket money; started off as a pound and gradually increased to £5, felt like I was a roller when this happened lol. Anyway, when my grandad passed away there was some strange happenings which I'd like to share with you. Bearing in mind I have no religion and think that when you're gone that's it. My grandad was convinced that he owed money to the council for poll tax or something and he would actively avoid talking to the authorities if he could help it. He had been taken into hospital ill, which was a regular occurrence throughout his life but this time for some reason he knew he was dying and had told my mom that he wanted to give his children and their partners a set amount of money (not loads but an amount each). My mom helped him sort this out and I believe that all of them got what he wished.

I saw him on his last day alive on earth (notice I didn't say on the day he died) and I was by now an adult(ish), the nurses told me that he had been saying he'd been seeing workmen on the building opposite that he could see from his bed and he asked me and my then girlfriend if we could see them. We couldn't but thought nothing of it, he then called me close and said to me, I haven't got a fiver for your pocket money, but have this bag of change, as far as I know it was his last lot of money that he took into the hospital, I said he didn't have to as I was well passed the age of the pocket money but as always he forced it into my had and gave me his stern but loving look. We finished our visit and looked again for the people on the roof that he could see, which we couldn't. That night he passed, and my girlfriend told me he was in the room with us. Of course, I shit my pants.

Later after it was all over, I counted the bag of change to take to the bank and there was exactly £5 in there which I thought was very weird and after that day, for about a month I found a £5 note once a week, like I was receiving pocket money from him. I also found a fiver the day after my wedding day and part of me likes to think it was him and my nan giving us a wedding present. Also, after seeing the film City of Angels with Nicholas Cage I wondered if the folks he was seeing on the building opposite were there to take him to the afterlife, or were they just delusions of a dying lovely old man? Also, it turned out that ironically, that the Council owed him money.

If you haven't got the meaning of this book yet, I'm not sure what to say but one more time, life is fucking short, sort stuff while you have the chance to like my grandad did perfectly. The above story is not to make you think there is an afterlife I very much doubt there is, but the message is to get your personal effects in order while you still can. Clear up any feuds with loved ones and tell people how you feel. Pay any debts off that you might have outstanding. Get your shit in order so the people left behind don't have anything to worry about and you can rest without worrying about what needs to be done. This also includes doing things for yourself, so you can look back and believe that you've had a good and fulfilling life, see bucket list chapter before this one. Time is ticking, you are dying from the moment you're born, if there's anything that needs doing bloody well do it before it's too late.

DYING Chapter 43

Blaze of Glory

Blaze of Glory – Bon-Jovi

'And of course death can't be conquered...but oh the battle can be glorious' PZ Myers

I wasn't as close to my nan on my dad's side as I was to my mom's side, primarily because my mom and dad weren't as close to them either but non the less when I got older and all of my other grandparents had passed away and my folks had moved to France, I visited her every other weekend. She used to offer me a Bailey's coffee when I got there. She used to drink a fair bit in fact, so much so that she used to get me to take her empty whisky and Baileys bottles back to mine to recycle so her sheltered accommodation didn't know how much she drank in a week lol.

She was nice, and we had a chatty relationship and I enjoyed my time visiting and talking about the past with her. She loved watching sport, one of my earliest memories was going to my nan and grandad's flat when my grandad was still alive and them watching a bright tv in a pitch-black room with snooker and horse racing on with the sound blasting out. It was loud because my granddad Ted was deaf and ironically was making my nan deaf due to the tv being on so loud and affecting her hearing. We used to sit there, and a whistling sound used to start coming from my grandad's ear and my nan would shout 'Ted' he'd reply 'ay?!' 'Ted' 'What?!' 'Ted you'm whistling!' 'ay?!', eventually he'd lip read and turn his hearing aid down which me and my dad would secretly find hilarious.

Anyway, my nan was my last grandparent to pass away and was probably the most psychologically fucked up experiences of my adult life (apart from when my uncle died obvs). My parents lived in France at the time so when she became ill I used to visit her on my own, it was ok at first but once she moved to a hospice, her health took a noticeable decline, which I guess is why people are moved to hospices. To begin with she would come to while I was there and I'd see a glimmer of my old nan below the surface, but gradually she declined from a slightly larger lady to a tiny foetus that didn't move but was still (technically) alive. For a couple of weeks, I would visit and sit there on my own looking at an immobile tiny withering human searching for the little old lady that I'd grown up with sitting on her lap, like some spectator at a freak show, waiting for something, anything to happen. This went on for some time and eventually she passed, and the whole experience made me realise that I never want my kids or grandkids or anyone for that matter to sit and watch me slowly curl up and die. I don't want my wife to have to wipe my bum (even though she said she would if I needed it).

The experience gave me more questions than answers. What were they keeping her alive for? To avoid sadness?

To reduce death statistics? Because they were legally bound to? Because it was illegal to end it for her? In case she had a miracle come back from this depleted state? I just couldn't and still can't get my head round it. After a pretty successful and happy life, she was kept barely alive to avoid the inevitable. Fuck that I'd like to go while I'm still able to walk and talk maybe shot by a marauding shooter, who didn't know me, and I didn't know them, clean and simple. I think I might need some psychological help after I've finished this book ha! I've also been writing a children's book while writing this, about a nana that's a ninja, I find myself needing less alcohol after working on those ones.

If you've never experienced someone dying that's close to you then you are lucky in a way but in another way, you are not so fortunate, because the end of someone else's life sharpens your focus to the beauty and wonder that is left of your own. I have seen three people that have died in the flesh, all of them I have loved and all of them upset me but the two that happened in my adult life made me realise the end is not so far away for all of us and the everyday worries about credit cards, flat tyres and work spats are as insignificant as a tiny mud patch on a football pitch so you should give them that amount of attention; zero or very little. I'm not saying I hope someone you know dies so you can experience the feeling but if and when you do you'll get what I mean, like a bucket of water over your head while sunbathing on a roasting hot day.

My TV is one of those smart digital things, I know I know that's not big news anymore because everyone has one but it's exciting to me so leave me be. For some reason when the TV is switched off and then on again it plays HD documentaries on a random channel that I've never heard of on a loop which can be rather annoying if you accidentally sit on the remote. One day, when I was shamefully doing fuck all, one of the looped documentaries that came on captured my attention. It was about extreme rock climbers and more interestingly, extreme tightrope walkers; guys that weren't happy with just climbing to massive heights, they then decided to walk across a cavern or between two mountains or whatever on a piece of wire. Nutters basically. So, while watching this junk TV, they interviewed one of the guys about his friend that had died undertaking the same random hobby as him, what he said has stayed with me ever since. When asked about the safety of the 'sport' and the risk of death he said, 'no one dies a noble death anymore' he would rather be doing what he loved than 'die an old person in a nursing home'. Deep, resonated a lot with my view of my nan's death.

I'm actually not advocating either of the above approaches; staying so safe that you wind up lifeless in a care home or be so fucking crazy that your chances of death multiply on a pissing hourly basis either! My view is that there is a happy medium to all of this (and I don't mean Derek Pakora lol) but what's the point in being so scared of your own shadow avoiding death and pain at all costs but missing out on life and what's the point in being so extreme that you end your fucking life before it's started causing pain and anguish to loved ones. In other words, having a death wish. My approach is to be brave, accept what comes your way, take calculated risks, check your safety ropes, assume you'll be fine and walk through life knowing that when death does come for you, you will have had a fulfilling life and there will be nothing to regret so then the fear of death is negated because there's nothing you needed to do before you go.

DYING Chapter 44

The First Rule of Death Club

Today – Smashing Pumpkins

'Yesterday's the past, tomorrow's the future, but today is a gift' that's why it's called the present' Bill Keane

A brilliant scene from one of my favourite films Fight Club was the one where Tyler Durden (Brad Pitt) holds up a liquor store. It wasn't unusual for his character to commit crime as he does so pretty much from the introduction of his character early in the movie. What is unusual is what unfolds, he takes the gas station attendant out to the forecourt and holds a gun to his head, while Edward Norton's character begs him to stop. He then takes the man's wallet and starts to read out the details of his driving licence. His name is Raymond K Hessall and he lives in a shitty flat, he then pulls out an expired student ID and Tyler asks why he no longer studies. Raymond confesses that he quit because school was too expensive, despite wanting to be a vet. Tyler then threatens to kill Raymond if he doesn't get back to school within 6 weeks before he allows him to run off. After that when Edward Norton questions him he states 'tomorrow will be the most beautiful day of Raymond K Hessall's life his breakfast will taste better than any meal you and I have ever tasted'.

This scene perfectly depicts what I am trying to tell you, stop wasting your life in lieu of something that is meaningless. Feel alive by respecting the fact that you will one day die. Edward Norton narrates just before 'on a long enough timeline, the survival rate for everyone drops to zero', each time I hear that line I get shivers, not only due to the excellent delivery from Norton but also it illustrates the bleakness of all of our futures and reminds me of the lack of respect we all have for the little time we have on the planet. So what have I been telling you to do? Do something meaningful.

Take a moment to think about this in the context of your life, have you abandoned your dreams for a shitty job? Have you stopped striving for your big goals for the easy option? Are you wasting time on social media or letting someone else plot the course of what you ultimately will end up doing? If you have, and Brad Pitt came into your place of work with a gun and dragged you out would you change? Would the motivation of someone threatening to kill you reignite your passion? If the answer is yes, visualise me or someone else turning up and threatening to kill you if you don't take back your life. Use this image and its subsequent motivation to give yourself permission to re-follow your dreams.

We only have today, yes that's right unlike the Bond film 'You Only Live Twice' I'm sad to say the Liam Gallagher track 'Once' where he said 'you only get do it once' is much more accurate. I know that you believe that there is a tomorrow (I do too) but when tomorrow gets there it's today again so if we are being completely scientific and accurate tomorrow doesn't actually exist, it's a concept that never arrives but allows us to keep things relative and surviving to the next bit after each section of darkness and sleep. Keep reminding yourself of this fact, because the one thing you haven't got is time to waste, what if today was your last, would you be pleased with what you've done? Have you celebrated your and others' existence, has it been a marvel to behold? Or did you have a crafty wank, eat last night's kebab and fall asleep to Netflix? Use your time wisely mofos as when the fat lady finally sings, as my good friend Dave says 'it's all over', you'll be underground or dust in the wind and all you'll have to show for it is a social media account that no one will look at and an internet history you wish you'd deleted. Stop pretending that watching the TV or scrolling through social media is doing something, actually do something. In fact, what are you doing reading this book? Do what my parents told me to do, fuck off and go outside and play with your mates. Do something, anything! Ps they didn't say 'fuck off' Lol.

Conclusion

You Are Going to Die!

We're on Our Way Now – Noel Gallagher

'I do not fear death. I had been dead for billions
and billions of years before I was born, and had not
suffered the slightest inconvenience from it'
Mark Twain

Yes, it's true. You are going to die, the sooner you
acknowledge this, the better. Place this book somewhere
you can see it and remind yourself regularly, daily if
you can. Take a picture of the cover and have it as your
phone background. Do whatever it takes to keep this
message at the forefront of your mind. And then...and
then nothing, live your life. Live life to the max as a
shameless ad for a cola I won't promote once said. By
having the knowledge of your mortality and everyone
else's mortality, you will be bullet proof (not literally!) in
the world as you know whatever you do eventually we
all pop our clogs and our life is as fleeting, as sure as

eggs is eggs (whatever that means) we are not leaving here alive and we should cherish our gift of life by living it for ourselves and not other people. Taking chances, dealing with losses, celebrating victories and laughing at hilarious jokes that make you snort pop out of your nose. Being born is out of our control and apart from general health and safety for the most part our death is out of our control too. It could be tomorrow, I hope it's not, it could be in a hundred years' time, nobody knows but the question I want you to ask yourself is, if it was tomorrow, have you lived enough up until now? Has today been up there with your best days of your life (excluding births or marriages)? Have you told the ones you love that you love them? Have you followed your dreams? Have you eaten your favourite foods? Have you done your favourite things to do?

As mentioned, at my work we follow the principles of the book; The Seven Habits of Highly Effective People, which were created by some clever chaps called Franklyn and Covey. One of the habits is 'Begin with the End in Mind'. Most of my organisation has taken this to mean start meetings or projects by describing what they'd like to achieve at the end of it and this is partly right, however my friend who's actually read the book has kindly informed me that the main meaning of the end is your death. It asks you to ask yourself how does what you're doing now impact the ending of your life. Kind of what I've been asking you to do all of the way through this book. How does Candy Crush or Tetris add to your ultimate life goals? What is it that you're not achieving by <insert your chosen distraction>?

My end in mind for writing this book is that I want you to have a really good life and I want you to be able to look back at the end of the book and your life and say 'that sweary bloke was right, I was and have always been going to die from the day I was born and by accepting this fact and even embracing it I have lived a fan bloody tastic life with love, joy, wealth and sadness so fuck you death, let's have it you fucking cunnnnnnnnnnnnnnnnt' in a Braveheart death stylee.

In the words of the Monty Python song at the end of the Life of Brian; Always Look on the Bright Side of Life – 'Always look on the bright side of death, just before you draw your terminal breath'. Think on.

Oh, and before I go, a big thanks to Captain Tom (now Colonel Tom) for inspiring me to get this done during lockdown well nearly, you are a true hero chap.

Lots of love,

AJ1

AJ1's Dadvice

(Random Life Tips)

Hello and welcome to the bonus mini book entitled 'AJ1's Dadvice', yes I know the patriarchy isn't 'cool' (I even did the uncool thing of doing inverted commas with my fingers), but I love my children, I love being a dad (most of the time) and it is my desire for my children to be better versions of me. This is why I never let them win at games, I always tell them how to do my magic tricks and am as much there for them as I can be despite one of them living in a separate house to me. During the writing of You Are Going to Fucking Die, I wrote some paragraphs that didn't quite fit the theme of the book but are pieces of advice that I would definitely like to pass on to my kids when they're older and some I have passed on to friends that have been struggling, and I thought that some of them might be useful for you guys too. These are meant as a guide **not** commandments, but they might prove useful to you (even if you discover you disagree with me) to work out some of this stuff for yourself. Like all good debates they lead to new thinking which is why I hope that society can recover from its current constant state of offence that it seems to be in. I hope that these help you.

LIFE TIP #1 – Everyone Wants Something (Even You!)

The slightly depressing fact is that everyone in your life is there due to something they want or need, and you are there for something that you want or need from them. The things wanted are probably not material, it is usually a social or economic desire but nonetheless almost all of our relationships are transactional. Our children live with us until they can provide for themselves (like birds leaving the nest). We may like spending time with someone who makes us feel special or intelligent or superior and we may shy away from someone that makes us feel inferior, guilty or bad. I am sorry to break this to you, but you are useful to someone until you are not. The same as people in your life are currently useful

224

to you until they are not. We are selfish creatures, as mentioned earlier; Darwin suggests that we only act in ways to ensure that our genes are passed on to the next generation. You may think that this is a bleak way of looking at our lives, but if you accept it you can also work out how you can maximise your relationships and even empower yourself to leave where there is something that you provide to someone else that is detrimental to you. If you are the butt of the jokes amongst friends then you provide humour to them, if this makes you feel like shit and you still go back, ask yourself what you are getting from them. Is it safety in numbers? Is it community? Is it a feeling of something to belong to or is it just that they provide something to do to avoid another (perceived) worse situation?

Gang studies have revealed that despite the increased risk of death, gang members appreciate the feeling of belonging or having a role model that they might not have received as a child. Think about that, there is an increased risk of death but paid off by the feeling of being part of a community. Armed with this knowledge, take the time to examine your relationships both good and bad, see what you're both taking away from it and decide if it is worth carrying on or not? I'm not saying ditch all of your friends and family because they might need a lift somewhere occasionally but do interrogate whether or not something is one sided or not.

LIFE TIP #2 – We ALL Have Mental Health

Like we all have physical health, we all have mental health. Some people have largely good mental health and some people at some points not so much. Don't arrogantly assume (like I did) that you are exempt from poor mental health just because you haven't experienced any yet. That's a bit like assuming because you haven't broken your leg yet that you never will. With this in mind go easy on yourself and others when it's obvious that their mental health needs a bit of a cast and a sling. Just don't offer to sign it! Lol.

LIFE TIP #3 – Small Positive Changes Lead to Big Changes

Ok so I think the title of this one is quite self-explanatory, but if you make small changes such as drinking one less beer or smoking one less cigarette, it will make large differences to your health over time. Same with saving money; if you can put a small amount of money away every month and not touch it, before long you will have a nice pot of money for a big purchase or a holiday further down the line. The trick is to get your mind to put off the short-term gain; spending now, mid-week beer, cheeky fag, extra chocolate bar and stave off for as long as possible in order to reach a benefit further down the line. Also, this can be come cumulative so if you start with little changes, these can grow when you can see benefits elsewhere. For instance, I didn't drink much in January and the positive feelings of doing that has made me want to drink less in general. Bonus! Apply this to anything that you're not happy with; doing a 5-minute walk per day is better than none, while you're out this might turn into ten minutes and so on. This is perfectly describing the compound effect which I will cover further in one of my future books.

LIFE TIP #4 – Don't Argue with People on the Internet

Society encourages us to be individual but in doing so do we become caught up in the thought that the world revolves around us? And then lose a grip of anyone else's perspective and in turn our altruism towards others? More and more I see people getting frustrated (and outraged) by things that other people have done or said irrespective of whether it is being said directly towards them. I mean how fucked up is that? When I

226

was a kid before social media existed, I knew that my parents disagreed with certain things their friends and family thought because they would talk about it in front of me. However, there was never any real arguments outside of a heated conversation with these people. My parents wouldn't dream of turning up at someone's door or phoning a stranger up to have a go at them about their beliefs, but this is what happens all of the fucking time on social media. In the same vain, no one, before social media would sit there watching two complete strangers argue over their differing opinions, which is what I do when I start reading the comments on Twitter and disappear down a rabbit hole for 20 minutes. Seriously, who gives a fuck what someone the other side of the street thinks, let alone on the other side of the world? Go back to living your life and chill the fuck out. One day you will die (that's what the main book is all about), do you really want to waste it arguing with strangers? Or worse accelerate the process by having a coronary while sitting on the pan looking at your phone and disagreeing with an equally deluded person?

If you're one of those that gets offended about everything and argues with strangers, please don't see this paragraph as a direct slur on you and turn up at my house in a ski mask and a bag of pool balls like Steven Segal. I don't know you and I didn't write it about you and if you think I did, seek help immediately or wake the fuck up and realise life isn't all about you, you fucking psycho!

LIFE TIP #5 – Don't Compare Yourself to Others – Be Yourself

In today's society we are surrounded by images of people that we are trying to be programmed to want to be like. The main reason for this is so that people can sell us shit, in other words; marketing. Whether it be in magazines, Instagram, films or TV ads they are trying to make you believe that to get (insert thing that you want here e.g. look beautiful/ handsome or be rich or I dunno have a bigger dick) you should buy X product that they're hawking. This has been true for years, hence why the Marlborough Man existed hence why David Beckham sells whisky, as far as I'm aware drinking Haig doesn't make you any better at fucking football. Anyway, this would be fine if this marketing hadn't become so insidious. They make people feel so bad about themselves that they want to be like someone so much that they forget that they themselves are beautiful too. You are beautiful, it may not be Angelina Jolie or Brad Pitt beauty, but I bet you are absolutely gorgeous to someone. It doesn't have to be external beauty either it could be your intelligence or lack thereof, it could be that you love rollercoasters, or you make brilliant cups of tea or you make someone laugh with crap jokes. Do not place people on pedestals and make yourself feel bad because they look good. Do not compare yourself to anyone else other than yourself and even then, only look for the improvements you can make to yourself. There are hundreds if not thousands of people that can be arse holes to you, don't be one to yourself. Life is like golf you're only playing against yourself. You are you and that's just brilliant in my book (literally it is my book!). Search for Bill Hicks marketing on YouTube if you'd like a laugh.

LIFE TIP #6 – Don't Take Anyone or Anything for Granted

It's easy to assume that the people and things that are there today will be there tomorrow. They were here yesterday and here today, so why wouldn't they be? Well things change, people's feelings change and the famous phrase 'shit happens' is also very true. I'm not saying feel completely on edge all of the time, like a coiled spring, but what I am advocating is to take stock of what you have got and don't assume that you can coast along in relationships without putting any effort into them.

LIFE TIP #7 – Don't Let People Take You for Granted

As a follow on from the last tip, if you're not treated well then don't hang around too long to see if it improves. You are the master of your destiny and if someone takes you for granted, tell them, give them a chance to change and if they don't, if you can, just leave.

LIFE TIP #8 – Remember Others Have Feelings Too

I'm as surprised as you that I've had to put this one in but the amount of horrible reviews and put downs I see on Amazon and social media it's like people have forgotten that they can refrain from commenting. Just because you're asked to review something doesn't give you the god given right to stick the knife in at the same time as the boot. People/ things may not have lived up to your expectations and it's fine to give an honest review but becoming abusive is just wrong and I'm sure you were bought up better than that. And if you weren't listen to your uncle Ad; you catch more flies with sugar than salt, so be kind.

LIFE TIP #9 – You Never Know Where You'll Find Happiness

This one I had to learn the hard way. I used to believe that I knew what would be good or bad to do, what would be enjoyable, but lockdown has made me realise that I took everything I could do outside my house for granted, that there would always be time to go here or there. I used to think I didn't like the cinema that much so only went occasionally now I wish I had gone every week because I can't go. You don't know what you've got til it's gone. The other part to this tip is that you never know what something is going to be like until you get there, this is so true. I have dreaded going places or meeting certain people and absolutely loved it when I went there or met them. Don't assume you have met all the best people or know your 'type of place' just fucking go wherever life takes you and see what these adventures bring to your view. You never know who you'll meet or what you'll do but if you don't go you'll never know!

LIFE TIP #10 – Never Beg

I don't mean never beg for money on the streets, although you should probably seek alternatives before you do. By 'never beg' I mean never beg someone to do something for you. I have begged twice for something in my life. The first time I got what I wanted, and it turned out to be terrible as the person resented me for them doing what I asked (stayed with me instead of splitting up) the second time I begged for something they completely ignored me and did what they wanted anyway and I just felt shit for having bared my soul to someone that didn't care. If you have to beg a person for something then it stands a chance that that person doesn't want to do what you are asking so it's best not to force them as a) it could be the wrong decision for them and it ends up coming back on you, and more importantly b) it could be the wrong decision for you because 'careful what you wish for, you might just get it' saying exists for a reason.

I know you think you know best for what you want but trust me, other people doing things to make you feel better is not the answer to your problem(s). Live for yourself, look for the reason behind what you think you need and solve that. I'll say it again, other people can't solve your issues, only you can. Also, as a footnote to all of the other reasons not to beg someone for something, it is also a big turn off to beg as you are showing weakness and desperation, our old pal Darwin suggests animals look for mates for the strength to provide, if you're showing that you need something from someone else it is automatically putting you at a position of weakness which is never a good sign and probably turning them off you at the same time. NEVER BEG ANYONE FOR ANYTHING!

LIFE TIP #11 – Get Enough Sleep

Oh man this is a biggy, the other week I got my audible credit and as I think I've mentioned before I do a lot of driving to pick my eldest son up. When I'm on my way to get him, I get through hours and hours of books and this time I had run out of authors and books to choose from and fancied a change. I asked on Rob Moore's Disruptive Entrepreneur group if anyone could recommend some new books and authors. One of the guys suggested 'Why We Sleep' by Matthew Walker. Well what can I say, thank you to the guy that suggested it. Walker explains how detrimental short or no sleep can be. It is linked to all manner of 'waking issues' and long-term problems. Getting too little sleep a night (less than 7 hours) over a long enough period of time can lead to obesity, memory loss, emotional damage and even dementia. Make sure you get enough sleep peeps and read/ listen to that book, you'll thank me for it.

LIFE TIP #12 – Be Kind (but Only if It's Reciprocated)

What's the point of being mean? Seriously meanies out there, what does it achieve? I can't see any real benefit. So why do we do it? I'm not saying be an angel and not take the piss out of each other, piss taking is fine as long as it's not too personal and it is going both ways. I mean why bully someone, why target one person and make their lives hell? Does it make your life any better?

No. So in the words of Adam Hills on the Last Leg 'stop being a dick!' But what if you don't know that you are being a dick, this is an interesting one. You may not have the self-awareness to realise, well firstly, do your friends dread you coming out or forget to invite you? Do you find yourself constantly targeting one person in your group? Do you ever make people cry? If you've answered 'yes' to any of these then you are probably the bully/ twat of your group. The next step is to catch yourself doing it. If and when you do, STOP, take a breath and apologise or if that's too hard just walk away and learn from that experience. You don't have to say the cruel thoughts despite what you've done in the past.

My one caveat for this tip is that you do not have to be kind and like everyone. If someone is a dick to you, you do not have to accept it. Just take yourself out of that person's life and move on. Remember the gang members staying despite the threat of death. If your group of friends or family for that matter make you feel like shit, find better people to spend your time with. They're out there, I promise.

LIFE TIP #13 – Don't Pin Everything on One Thing

Remember the phrase don't put all your eggs in one basket, well I can attest that it's true. Not everything works out, relationships fail, careers or jobs aren't always the best move, but if you pin your hopes or define/ design yourself based on one thing making you happy or one concept of success then you are increasing your chances of being unhappy. During a dark relationship period I believed that only one girl could make me happy. I focused on her so much that I lost her, don't be that guy. Spread your interests, have an open mind to other hobbies or careers, don't just assume that the one thing your chasing is the ONLY thing to chase. Also, the danger of focusing on one idea of yourself makes you rigid for when change inevitably comes, if you only picture yourself as an athlete, what if say an illness comes along that affects your fitness and ability to compete, perhaps not even an illness it could just be the inevitable old age that gets us all. You'll be more devastated than if you had lots of different interests or at least an open mind to doing something else with your life.

LIFE TIP #14 – Know Your Own Worth

I am about to say the second factual thing in this book after the fact that you will die. You are the best you in the world! You are the best you ever! Why? Because there is only one and will only ever be one of you! This is the only life, body, personality, brain that you've got and will have so DO NOT BE ASHAMED OF WHO YOU ARE! Embrace your curves or exercise, admit to being thick or educate yourself so you're less thick, pluck your mono brow or Oasis-it-up, it doesn't matter. No one really cares what you do as long as it doesn't affect them. Be proud of who you are and if the people around you don't like it tell them to fack awf! One day you will die, what's the point in waiting and dreaming to be different for other people when you can go out and live a life today exactly as you are. Be loud, proud and fuck the crowd!

LIFE TIP #15 – Don't Be Too Proud to Ask for Help

There is no pressure to know everything, there is no responsibility to be good at anything, there are only the rules and expectations that you set yourself. I have found throughout my life that when I've tried to go things alone, I ultimately fail and guess what? It feels like absolute shit. My son is going through that age where if he's not good the first time at something he doesn't want to try again because he thinks he's bad at it. I go to great lengths to tell him that even the professionals in a particular sport or activity had a first time at their craft and were probably rubbish, the only difference with them is that they kept at it, the other thing I point out to them as that the professional almost definitely has a coach and probably has a mentor. If it's good enough for these folks, why isn't it good enough for me or you? Ask for help, but just make sure the person that you're asking has some experience (and success) in what you want to achieve.

Remember free advice is worth every penny, so don't be afraid to pay someone or at least make it worth their while to help you. If they are good your initial outlay will be returned to you in scores.

LIFE TIP #16 – Love People but Don't Expect It Back

Ever heard the phrase love like you've never had your heart broken? I like this phrase, but I think it needs a little more explaining. I have been in love a few times in my life and I have had people that I think that I have been in love with. I loved them so much when they told me that they didn't love me back, I wanted to tell the police because it felt like such an injustice lol. But what I have realised is that loving someone without expecting anything back is a much healthier approach however, I acknowledge that this is quite hard. If you expect something back and it's not reciprocated this can be disappointing, heart breaking in fact. Far be it from me to exclaim expertise in the matters of the heart but my advice is to approach any relationship with an open mind, remember the other person has wants, needs and expectations that may be different to what you can provide. You may find love as friends but if it's not meant to be it's not meant to be. Don't become a super weird stalker if they decide that a relationship with you is not for them (also see tip about never begging).

LIFE TIP #17 – Fortune Favours the Patient

Have patience. If you plant a seed in the garden today and go out tomorrow morning and there's no tree or plant would you immediately phone the garden centre to complain? No of course you wouldn't so why do we as humans get so disheartened if we can't get something, do something or don't achieve something straight away. We are so short sighted about how long things take to do, if at first you don't succeed try again. Fail fast and adjust. I will be writing a book on this very topic, so I won't spoil it by squeezing it all in one tip. There you go, an opportunity for you to be patient.

LIFE TIP #18 – Failure Is the Only Way to Become Awesome

Despite how failure makes you feel when it happens, it is actually a positive thing to help you achieve your goals. Every successful person in a particular field started out as an amateur, a novice, a beginner whatever you want to call it. David Beckham didn't play his first football match and score a perfect free kick. It is only through playing and practicing that he honed his skill and got good. Of course, a bit of natural talent, supportive parents and financial stability helps but the old adage practice makes perfect is true. But for every successful goal on target there were probably hundreds of failed attempts that we never get to see or remember from boring matches and practices. This hidden failure is overlooked when we see him being awesome on the pitch and can cause us to assume we are terrible when we first try something. I passed my driving test on my third time, I was gutted because I was desperate to drive, but looking back after driving 24 years, that was all about teaching me to drive correctly, not a reflection on my self-worth and it was also only a relatively small time in the grand scheme of things. Be the one that fails!

LIFE TIP #19 – Get Shit Done Even if It Sucks

There is a sense of satisfaction at the completion of a hard or shitty piece of work. By quitting mid-way through you deny yourself this feeling of accomplishment. Some of the hardest things I've ever done are now the backbone to most of my anecdotes in this book. A good saying that I like is 'you only regret the things you didn't do' and this is so true for me. I look back at some of the times I have given up and wished now that I could go back and encourage myself to continue, despite the pain, sadness or frustration it was causing me at the time.

LIFE TIP #20 – Meditation Is Awesome

Yes, there I said it, blokey blokes out there, don't worry it's not a reflection of your manhood, you don't have to wear Lycra, drink fruit tea and I promise your dick won't drop off if you meditate, well mine hasn't anyway. I decided to start meditating when I was going through a particularly shit time in my life, I had some crap thoughts and had seen in films that people meditated to calm their mind. As I was living in Tipton when I wanted to test it out, I shut the curtains, so everyone thought I was masturbating as that was more socially acceptable. I started just looking at YouTube videos and followed different poses to try to help me focus but I can tell you, sitting alone in silence with your eyes closed is all you need to do. Try it for a few minutes and do it every day and you will get better over time (like everything else you want to get good at actually). I'm not sure how it works but this time out really clears my mind and gets me out of my shitty moods when I need to, gives me new ideas if I need one and basically just gives my brain a makeover to tackle the rest of the day. If you can find 5 minutes to meditate which I'm sure you can, you won't regret it. Consider it a little gift to yourself.

LIFE TIP #21 – Have Quiet Time

This is not a repeat of the last tip. This is about having some time not doing anything not even meditating. We currently have access to hundreds of billions of forms of distraction through the power of the internet, some healthy and some that aren't that good for us or maybe even downright destructive. But it's not just the obvious social media and games on our phones we also have streaming TV with 24/ 7 access, Kindle and Audible with unlimited books, learning websites and many many more that I'm probably not aware of because I'm an old fart. Anyway, you get my point, compared to when I was a kid and we had four tv channels, no phones and no video player, there were really quiet afternoons where would just colour in or play with toy soldiers. I know this sounds boring, but the quietness of the play was very relaxing, and I think that our senses need a break and our imaginations need a bit of a run out too. If you can sit and chill for half an hour without speaking to anyone (in person or on a device) or without playing a video game, watching TV, reading a book or listening to music your mind will appreciate it once it has realised you haven't gone blind and deaf. Perhaps you could do a mindful colouring book. Essentially this tip is all about learning to enjoy your own company without reaching for your phone at the first inkling that you might have to be alone.

LIFE TIP #22 – Only Care about People's Opinions When It Counts

In the age of social media everyone has a fucking opinion on everything, but do you ever stop and think that if these people know so much about what's going on, why aren't they in any position of power to actually impart this knowledge in a place where it could actually do some good? In the past, I have let people tell me that I am not good at something especially in an artistic sense because I wasn't very confident (yeah seriously) and was constantly seeking reassurance. Listening to feedback is fine and can be helpful but you also have to remember to check the person's credentials that are giving the feedback. Firstly, are they your chosen audience? Secondly, have they achieved what you are trying to successfully do, in their life? Thirdly, what is their motivation for giving you this feedback? Is it from a good place to help you or is it to stop you from continuing so they don't feel bad about their achievements or lack thereof? Looking back at some of the feedback I've received in the past about my band, if I'd have paused and asked myself those three questions I would have thought less about their opinion and not let it affect me so much like I did back then.

I would also encourage you to err on the side of caution when it comes to positive feedback. Some people just really like you and in trying to make you feel good will say things that they may not necessarily feel and give you a false sense of security. We've all seen the crazy families on X-factor that have bigged their kid up so much they just can't accept that she's not that good. Also, some people are just too nice and will give compliments instead of what they really think which can also give you a misleading impression of your talent/ skill.

Both positive and negative feedback should come second to your thoughts and feelings about an endeavour. Remember that and you'll be fine regardless of what they say and if it makes you happy and you're not hurting anyone carry on doing it champ!

LIFE TIP #23 – Don't Seek Praise and Reassurance from Social Media

Social media has become a pastime and can be quite addictive. It has gone from something that you occasionally post your holiday snaps on to a full-blown attack on the senses. There's so much in there as we tweet and retweet and retweet someone else's retweet that it is easy to get dragged down a rabbit hole and not come out for hours missing good chunks of your life and possibly conversations and opportunities to do actual things. The engulfing nature of this means that it has potential to dictate your reality. There has been a couple of times where I have had to step away for a while (social media-isolate lol) and one of my good friends has gone off grid completely to avoid the stress of the social media merry-go-round. I'm not entirely against it but if you are posting to seek reassurance you may be disappointed, just because people do or don't like something doesn't detract or indicate whether something is good or not. If you value this opinion too much you will end up shaping what you do and then post to attract the post likes and end up being a shell of your former self in order to fuel this 'like addiction'. Put the phone down and chat to the real people in your life before you become a boring wet fart.

LIFE TIP #24 – Don't Piss on Other People's Chips (Literally and Figuratively)

Firstly, just don't piss on anyone's chips, it's not vinegar so don't do it! Also, when giving feedback and by this, I mean the negative kind do you ever stop and think where your motivation is coming from? If it is from a good place to help the other person to succeed, then great just be sensitive in your delivery. If it is from a place of wanting to stop them or slow them down from achieving something you may be jealous of then you need to stop being a dick. Success isn't a finite resource, by someone having success doesn't stop someone else getting their own share of success. Two people can be successful at the same time e.g. Nike and Adidas were two brothers. They are both successful and continue to be so. They exist in the same world and the people you know can be successful and won't detract from your potential. You are both on individual paths and if you feel the need to block someone else's path then that makes you a twat and you should rethink this approach to life. If you support them they will be more appreciative, and this positivity will a) make you feel good and b) potentially bring good shit into your world too.

LIFE TIP #25 – Take Calculated Risks

One of Rob Moore's famous catchphrases is 'if you don't risk anything, you risk everything', I like this because most parents (including mine) teach their kids to not take risky paths. This is true for certain things like don't take your new bike and risk leaving it outside the shop without its chain on. However, this advice gets embedded and we become risk averse adults but it's no longer just our bikes that we worry about. My concern is that people are so scared of failing that it paralyses them in to not doing anything outside of what they already know. My advice is (and is similar to the theme of this book) look at the risk and work out if the action if unsuccessful would kill you versus what potential rewards you would get by taking the risk. Live a little.

LIFE TIP #26 – Do Not Set Foot in a Casino/ Bookmakers

As a former croupier and former gambling addict, I feel that I am in a pretty good space to let you know that no positives come from gambling in the long run. Again, this is probably fuelled from the impatient/ get rich quick idea of getting money and ultimately what you want without working hard for it. You may get a rush from a few wins but from a long-term perspective, unless you are very good at controlling your urges and walking away when you win or lose (like my best friend is grr!) you will ultimately lose, and the casino/ book makers will ultimately win. Don't believe me, sit outside your local bookies that has a cashpoint nearby and watch the poor bastards coming out when they lose to get more money to feed their addiction, and chasing their money. I was one of them and it's a fucking shit life!

LIFE TIP #27 – Don't Like Something Just because Other People Do

There's a worrying trend at the minute where it is cool to like or dislike what other people like or dislike especially in social media, I believe the young kids call it 'trending' lol. This is fine on a microlevel but when it comes to big political newsworthy issues this can be divisive and potentially very dangerous. Think for yourself not just what hash tag is trending on Twitter today. Think for yourself dumb fucks because I told you to lol!

LIFE TIP #28 – Don't Ask Someone to Do Something You Wouldn't Do Yourself

I've had some shitty managers in the past, I've also had some brilliant ones, especially my good friend and colleague Mick, who made his team feel like a little family, so it was a pleasure to go in every day (and so I did, even when I was ill!). I've been a manager too and the thing I've found that made me respect my manager and made my direct reports respect me is to never ask them to do something that I wouldn't do myself. This will put you in good stead, because if they see you get your hands dirty you go from manager to leader in their eyes and will get more respect from them as they know that what your asking is (most likely) reasonable and if you will do it there's no reason they shouldn't. If you're the type of manager that just constantly delegates the shit jobs, then you'll get back shit attitudes and support from the people who work for you. My dad was a bakery engineer and was once asked by a manager that he didn't like to do something he didn't think he should be doing, my dad smiled, and the manager asked why? My dad said to him 'I can run, or I can walk, and you won't know the difference' knowing full well that the manager couldn't do what he could do and could lead him on a merry dance if he didn't respect his knowledge of the machines that he worked on. Think on that.

LIFE TIP #29 – Give to Charity/Leave Waiter & Waitress Tips

You might think that by not giving to charity or leaving tips that you are saving yourself money. This is true to a certain extent however, in my experience (and according to money gurus) the more you give the more it comes back to you in other ways. The movement of money makes you feel positive about money, and if you feel you have enough to give to someone that will benefit from it, the universe helps fulfil that back to you. This is having an abundance mentality. If you have money but feel like you're too poor to donate, then I'm sorry to say you have a scarcity mentality and while you feel like this, you will always feel too poor and your world will always reflect this back to you. Stick your hand in your pocket, you can't take it with you after all. Don't be Mr. Pink in Reservoir Dogs.

LIFE TIP #30 – No One Can Live Your Life for You

As much as we'd all like someone else to do everything for us, the joy and rewarding feelings are in the achievement of something special not someone else doing it for you.

LIFE TIP #31 – Don't Live Your Life Through Someone Else

Pushy parents stop right now! Your kids aren't there to re-enact what you wanted to achieve they are there to live their own lives whatever they may choose it to be. Deep down you know if this is your dream or theirs and if it's yours give it a rest as they'll only end up resenting you later on in life. If you share your interest that's fine they may grow into liking it and be your partner in crime but if you push them they will push back eventually. Also, if they do achieve it begrudgingly; neither of you will feel the benefit of the experience because a) it won't be you there winning the Olympic Gold or whatever and b) their victory will be empty as it's not their passion to begin with its bloody yours ya big arse. If you want to achieve something do it for yourself, it's never too late to be awesome, look at Colonel Tom!

LIFE TIP #32 – Read Books

Read and learn as much as you can, every piece of knowledge will help you along the way. Knowledge is power. At the same time put what you learn into action by putting the books down and experiencing life too.

LIFE TIP #33 – Don't Believe Everything You Read or See on the News

Just for a moment I am going to put my tinfoil hat on sorry. And I know this is slightly contradictory to the last tip. But I just wanted to let you know or maybe remind you that most media outlets have shareholders, partners and benefactors. Not everything you read or see on any of the news channels is without bias. Also, sometimes the bias is purposely there in order to generate hate to the other side of the agenda in order to create and mobilise change which may not always be to your or the other listeners/ readers/ watchers benefit. Try to view news with a cautious eye.

LIFE TIP #34 – School Is Not Everything

It is fine for you to want your children to have good academic achievements, as long as you don't place too much importance on it over and above life experience and natural talent. School up until college years really only teaches all of the children the same knowledge, it's what you can teach them that is unique that will set them apart from the herd.

LIFE TIP #35 – Make Exercise Your Habit

Unless you are a completely random nutcase, your life is most likely made up of a number of habits both good and bad whether you know this or not is a different story. The word 'habit' to me always springs to mind something bad like smoking but habits are much more than this. Google dictionary says a habit is 'a settled or regular tendency or practice, especially one that is hard to give up'. So, if you get up every day at 8am and then hit the snooze button til 8.15am, that's a habit. If you have cereal for breakfast every day that's a habit, our clothing style is a habit. You see where I'm going most things that you do and make up your daily life are habits. I, like most people have positive and negative ones, off the top of my head a positive one, is checking how my children are every day either in person, by text or on Facetime, a negative one that I have is drinking too much craft beer. Exercise has never been a strong one for me but as midlife has dawned on me I have noticed that I need to do more to keep fit. During the lockdown period I started to do the Joe Wicks PE sessions to keep fit as I wasn't going outside and walking about like usual. I really enjoyed them and got into a habit of doing it. It made me feel brilliant as according to Wicks on his YouTube channel the act of exercise releases positive endorphins (the happiness chemical that's also released by chocolate) which in turn makes you feel good. However, I only stopped for 3 days and I lost the momentum and lost the habit. A good book on habits is called Atomic Habits by James Clear, he describes in lots of detail how to embed positive habits and remove or lessen negative ones.

LIFE TIP #36 – Look after Your Body

This is your vessel, your ship, your shell, the only one this version of you will ever have. Value it, keep it safe and go easy on it because as we've learnt your life is precious and if you fuck it up it will hinder how much you can do.

LIFE TIP #37 – Moaning Doesn't Change Anything

I fucking hate moaning bastards. Not necessarily because they moan but because they assume that moaning actually achieves something (and I am interested in it!). You ever heard anyone say, 'ooh I love a good moan', yep plenty? You ever heard anyone say, 'I can't wait to listen to such and such moan'? No because no fucker has ever said it because no one *really* wants to hear it! Why? Because it DOESN'T CHANGE A FUCKING THING. My wife gets annoyed with me the day after I've been out drinking, she can see I blatantly have a hangover because I look like death warmed up but because I know there's nothing anyone can do about it except wait out the shivers and the puke, I always say 'I'm fine' and never admit that it may be something called the dreaded 'hangover'. I just don't see the point in saying it, if anything I feel that if I say it aloud it's got more chance of getting worse, where if I just try to get on with my life as well as I can it'll get better quicker. I'm not saying don't get pissed off when something doesn't go your way or confide in someone

245

about it, but what I am saying is that the quicker you can dust yourself off and move on the quicker you'll feel better and probably get somewhere like where you wanted to achieve in the first place.

LIFE TIP #38 – Snap It/Record It/Journal It

Me and you are so lucky that we have our lives in a time where we are relatively safe, life expectancy is high, and entertainment is in abundance. We also live in a time where acceptance of differences is quite high too although the far left and right would have you believe otherwise. Life moves fast, and before you know it, it will be gone or at least this moment will. Make sure you photograph or video the good times (in moderation of course), so you can look back and remember it. My memory is not so great thanks to my old pal beer and having the photos of good times helps jog my memory. Also, if you have the patience, to type or pick up pen and paper, journal what you are experiencing whether it be good or bad, so you can reflect on what you've learnt along the way, remember the good times and appreciate when the bad times have passed. I journal sporadically and wish I could do it more consistently, though I have found these books to be quite a good journal as you've probably noticed I stick a load of my personal experiences and anecdotes in them so when I'm old and grey(er) I can have a read about what happened to me. You are the story, live it, like it record it (but don't video every-fucking-thing as per my statement earlier about recording gigs etc).

LIFE TIP #39 – No Such Thing as Can't

You've probably picked up that I'm a pretty proactive guy, and this has always been the case with the occasional blip of laziness or apathy. My pet hate is hearing someone say that they can't do it. As Yoda says 'do or do not, there is no try' which is so true. I believe that anyone can pretty much do anything with practice and time. To say you can't, is (mostly) a cop out and I try to discourage my kids (and some close loved ones around me) from saying it, the language we use influences the outcomes of our approach to life. If you don't want to do something then that's a different matter, don't fucking do it and tell me that you don't. But if you want to do it, and have no physical reason not to do something and you say you can't do it then you should slap yourself in the face. And if you say you can't do that then I will do it for you.

LIFE TIP #40 – Avoid Debt Like the Fucking Plague

Yes, you love buying shit, I do too. Yes, you love having new shit, me too! Yes, it's good to have the latest whatever and look like Billy Big-Bollocks (not a real person) but if you spend money that you haven't got you are probably going to have to get into debt. Borrowing money that is not already yours before you've earned it is a one-way ticket to Shitsville Arizona, USA (not a real place). Credit cards and loans start off great, ooh I'll just get this, and I'll pay it back when I get paid, however, these companies are banking (get it) on you forgetting, buying more shit and borrowing more dough, getting into trouble, all so they can rape your ass hole dry. I'm sorry to be so rude (in this instance) but it's so true. Make do with what you've got, every cheap ass phone now has a camera, texts and calls keep using the one you've got. If you can't afford a car use public transport until you can buy a cheap one and work your way up (be patient, see next tip). The only exception to this is a mortgage which is 'good debt' where it is more of a borrow to invest than a borrow for shit that will lose its value such as phones, clothes, cars and other dross I can't be arsed to think that you buy.

LIFE TIP #41 – Don't Be in Too Much of a Rush

Kind of following on from the last tip, I feel that each generation has a desire to be more adult than the last. Kids smoking to look older, getting fake IDs to buy alcohol etc, and this seems to be true in the workplace nowadays. All of the young and attractive peeps desperate for the next promotion and I'm guessing next pay rise. Perhaps I was like this too, I was quite an eager beaver out of university but all I'll say for this one, is when you earn more you are expected to do more and be more responsible for stuff, to the point where I wish I was back on by £18k a year job where no one gave a shit if I turned up pissed and puked in a bin. The extra money just gets eaten up into buying more things and you're just having to run faster on the merry go round to speed up. I'm not saying don't strive for promotions and indeed being top of your game, but you have loads of years to get there so be young and enjoy yourself while you have little or no responsibility.

LIFE TIP #42 – Everyone Takes the Piss

When you're a kid, most of us live in a utopia where no one takes the piss out of you for anything because they're your family. A happy safe little bubble of joy, then you get to senior school and unless you're Charlie Bronson you're getting the piss taken out of you big time, then you go to work more piss taking and if you're brave enough to go out with a group of girls or lads on a stag do/ hen do/ piss up the piss will be well and truly absorbed from your very soul. For a good number of years, I fought against this, assuming I could return to my haven that my family gave me. WRONG! It never happens, the sooner that you and your kids realise that people take the piss the sooner that you can accept it and not let it affect you so much. I am a sensitive soul believe it or not, so I get hurt occasionally from a close piss taker but in the long run you and I have to realise that everyone takes the fucking piss. Now, if someone is bullying you because it's only you being taken the piss out for personal reasons then you need to smack that cunt down or at the very least leave the scenario.

LIFE TIP #43 – Remember Anyone You Meet Could Be Going Through Shit

There are some people at work who really piss me off, I'm sure there's probably people at your work or in your life who really piss you off too. Even though they might be the biggest knob head in the world remember that they are people too, they might have shit going on at home and deserve to have a baseline level of decency given to them. Also, I read a great quote the other day about bullies I think it was for black lives matter or something like that and it went something like 'I will not disrespect myself by responding to your behaviour in the same way that has offended me'. I really like the sentiment here because the phrase two wrongs don't make a right is so true. What's the point in me flaring up back to someone who is probably only acting like that because they're hurting from something, let's face it that can be the only reason they'll be doing something to hurt someone else. They need to realise that by hurting someone else doesn't sort their own shit out. I don't think I came up with the previous sentence but hopefully no one is going to sue me.

LIFE TIP #44 – Use Your Vote

Ok yes this may seem a boring one, but you really should use your vote when given the opportunity. It is one of the main ways you can influence the things that happen in the world. I'm not saying who you should vote for that's down to your own politics but lots of people have fought and died for you to be able to go to that voting booth. You may even choose to ruin your vote (I have once!) but still go, as if you just let the vote pass without having a say then you do not have the right to complain when things happen to you that you do not like. Boring party-political broadcast over. Let's move on quickly!

LIFE TIP #45 – Don't Talk Politics with Friends

Oh, shit it's a follow up on the last tip, but a quite straightforward one so humour me. Different people have different views, sometimes they will be different and sometimes they may be the same as you. If you value your friendships keep the topic from your conversations as you can lose friends unnecessarily.

LIFE TIP #46 – Some People Are Actually Just Fucked

My parents did their best at raising me to be polite to everyone, open doors for anyone and stand up for pregnant women or little old ladies (or gents) on the bus. Great. But there are situations where this is not so great. Why? Because there are some people that are called psychopaths, sociopaths and narcissists that do not give a fuck about my (or your) politeness or good deeds and they only care about pleasing and amusing themselves. You shouldn't hate them for this as they can't actually help it, some are born this way and there was nothing that their folks could do to prevent it, and some could have been prevented but the right interventions weren't put in place by parents or guardians. What you do need to do, is temper how much time you give them and how much of their opinion slash bullshit that you take on board. In contrast to most of society they are fucked up and can make you feel like the fucked up one because they will have no problem being mean to you despite how well you've been taught to treat people. Do not let them get to you. You now know that there are these peeps out there and when you occasionally

250

find someone that goes against the grain, don't do what I did and try to gain respect from them, run away as fast as you can as it's only you that will get hurt in that scenario. See the BBC drama Killing Eve for more information on this.

LIFE TIP #47 – Revenge Is a Waste of Time

Yep they've stole or broke your boy/ girl/ car/ gnome whatever and you're super fucking pissed. I get it I really do, I have a reasonably short fuse for unfairness. For five minutes after shit has happened I plot the murder and subsequent burying of whoever has done the dirty on me. I then chill the eff out and realise that it is pointless to go and key their car or whatever because a) they won't know its me so they have no clue why it's happened to see it as 'justice' to reflect up on it b) if they did know it was me it continues the cycle of shit as they look to take revenge back and c) they probably didn't do it to intentionally fuck you off and if they did do it on purpose to genuinely piss you off then they are a probably a psychopath (see previous tip) and you should be running. Just assume they're a knob head, ignore, forgive, forget and fuck it!!!! The less anger in your life the healthier your mental wellbeing and the less shit you'll put in your body as a result.

LIFE TIP #48 – Problems Lead to More Problems

An unfortunate fact of life is that other people exist lol. But what I mean by this is that when you have a problem (as we all do) you work on solving it which is great. However, you assume that by solving that problem that things will be fine and there will be less problems, unfortunately this is not the case and your next problem then becomes your focus. Rob Moore says something along the lines of don't try and remove problems, just try to attract better ones.

LIFE TIP #49 – Keep Going

I can't pretend that life is easy it isn't, some days will be hard as fuck, you will experience all manner of pain and suffering before you die but there will also be moments of pure happiness too. This is the yin and yang of life, you can't have one without the other. The trick is to keep going no matter what is happening, Winston Churchill said, 'if you're going through hell, keep going' and he's right. Do not make permanent decisions when things are shit, just focus on the light at the end of the tunnel.

LIFE TIP #50 – The Basics

Quick list of do's and don'ts.

Do learn to swim (it could save your life)
Do learn to drive (it helps you become independent)
Do be kind to others (obvious one)
Do drink lots of water
Do say please and thank you (manners cost nothing but mean everything)
Do help others if you're able
Do look up from your phone when you see someone you know
Do try to be open minded when it comes to the opinions of others

Don't smoke (anything you set on fire and put in your mouth can't be good for you)
Don't drink too much (it's poison)
Don't eat too much junk food but don't starve yourself either
Don't discriminate against anyone (we all have a different perspective of life)
Don't drink and drive (could fuck up loads of lives not just your own)
Don't stop your kids from dreaming big
Don't stop dreaming big yourself

Don't make being famous your only goal (you will probably be disappointed even if you get it)
Don't judge the actions of others too harshly, we're all trying our best

LIFE TIP #51 – You Got This

No book will give you all the answers, though I hope I have given you some food for thought. Regardless of what anyone says to you, your wellbeing and life are in your hands because you have the freedom to choose what you think and feel about the situation that you are in, and the power to act accordingly if it's not what you want. I may as well finish with a quote from Captain Jack Sparrow in Pirates of the Caribbean, 'the problem is not the problem, the problem is your attitude about the problem'. You have got this and if you haven't go and bloody get it!

THE END (That's all folks!)

For more *ahem* words of wisdom visit my Instagram page @aj1books where an internet elf called Beckie transforms my brain farts into professional looking memes.

FREE Cut Out Memento Mori

YOU ARE GOING TO F*CKING DIE

Adam Jones

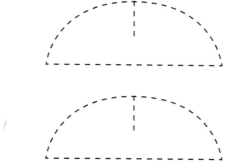

Printed in Great Britain
by Amazon

73018175R00154